Forming FAITH in a Hurricane

A Spiritual Primer for Daily Living

Forming FAITH in a Hurricane

A Spiritual Primer for Daily Living

N. Graham Standish

FORMING FAITH IN A HURRICANE
A Spiritual Primer for Daily Living

The Upper Room Web Site: http://www.upperroom.org

Cover design: Jim Bateman
Cover transparency: R. Dahlquist/SuperStock
First printing: 1998

Library of Congress Cataloging-in-Publication

Standish, N. Graham, 1959– .
Forming faith in a hurricane / N. Graham Standish.
p. cm.
ISBN 0-8358-0848-3
1. Spiritual formation. I. Title.
BV4501.2.S7156 1998 97-23358
248.4—dc21 CIP

Printed in the United States of America

For their support and care,
I thank my parents.
For their love despite my faults,
I thank my brothers and sisters.
For her beauty, wisdom, optimism, and love,
I thank my wife, Diane.

You are altogether beautiful, my love;
there is no flaw in you.

—Song of Solomon 4:7

Contents

Introduction

FORMING A STRONG FAITH, while never easy in any period of history, seems especially difficult today. Many aspects of our present culture make it hard for us to form a strong faith. Throughout history, Christians have faced the persecutions of Rome, the darkness of the Middle Ages, the uncertainty of the Reformation, and the divisiveness of religious wars; yet they still lived in religious cultures. They may have had to choose between one religious system or another, but religion was a major part of their daily lives. True atheism—the rejection of God and the divine—has only become a common belief over the past 200 years. For centuries, Christians have lived in cultures and societies that took religious belief—be it Christian or another tradition—seriously.

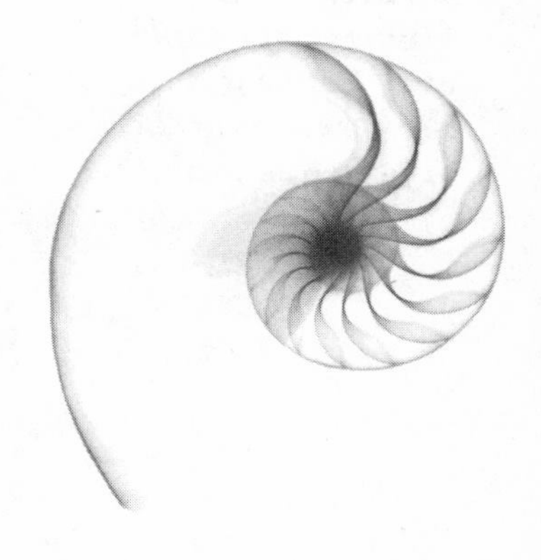

Today we live in a culture that questions faith continually. While direct attacks on faith and religious belief occur on rare occasions, our culture attacks faith in more subtle and insidious ways. It attacks religion by making all religious practices seem relative. Our culture does not destroy faith directly; it erodes faith little by little. For instance, Sunday used to be a day of rest and worship. Today it is much like any other day. Prayer groups, Bible studies, and worship used to be central activities in many communities. Today these practices are central only for some people. The decline in practice of faith does not mean that we should return to earlier times, but it points out that cultural practices and beliefs have slowly eroded the centrality of faith in people's lives.

For centuries, Christians have lived in cultures and societies that took religious belief seriously.

Faith is also difficult for us today because we live in a fast-paced, overstimulated culture that demands more and more of our time and attention. Computers, originally hailed as technological advances to simplify our lives, have had the opposite effect. Computers now demand more of our time as they help us create more and more information. Information rushes at us so quickly that we have little time to digest it. I know a lawyer who told me that the widespread use of fax machines has stolen much of his free time. In contrast to the way he conducted his business ten years ago, his associates and clients can now wait until the very last minute to complete projects. They often fax documents to him at the end of a workday and expect him to review them overnight. He says that the mountain of papers he receives by fax at 4:30 on Friday afternoons from people who want a reply by early Monday morning has compromised his time of rest on the weekend. This "last-minute" capability has increased his workload in the evenings and the weekends. As a result, his religious life and faith have suffered. He worries that he now serves work, not God, and that he has little time for prayer and reflection.

Churches feel called to respond to the spiritual needs and hungers of people who "want it all," while resisting the urge to "be it all."

In addition, people today feel compelled to "do it all." We devote tremendous amounts of energy to success in the workplace, time with our children, and time off in leisurely activities. We move in so many different directions and respond to so many different demands that matters of faith and spirituality seem like luxuries that we can include in our lives only if we find the time —maybe tomorrow, next week, next month, next year. One woman with two small children told me that between work, taking care of the children, and finding time for herself, she just did not have the time to go to church and "worry about all that stuff."

Churches often add to this fast-paced dilemma. Many churches feel the need to offer something for everyone: a great children's education program, a vibrant youth ministry, an active adult education program, enthusiastic and effective boards and committees, creative fellowship opportunities, and strong mission efforts. All of these components require intensive participation by church members, which can take away from time spent with families, friends, and oneself. Churches feel called to respond to the spiritual needs and hungers of people who "want it all," while resisting the urge to "be it all." Church participation is important, yet our fast-paced culture can lead to fast-paced churches that add to the daily stress many members experience.

In addition to the drain that a hurried culture can have on our faith and spirituality, we also live in a cautious and skeptical culture that is hesitant about religious commitments. Many people in our culture view religion either as an anachronism or as a crutch for overly dependent people who cannot think for themselves. Added to this perception is the fact that now we have produced two generations of people (the "baby-boom" and "X" generations) who have learned to approach commitment—religious, relational, vocational, social, and political—cautiously. All of these demands and stimulations can blow through our lives at gale force, making it hard to form a strong faith. They blow us off our foundations. If we are to take forming a strong faith seriously, then we must keep in mind several notions about faith.

Faith is not something we have; it is a journey we take.

1 While we tend to think of faith in static terms, *faith is always a process*. Faith is not something we have; it is a journey we take. Many Christians believe that we can capture faith and quantify it. People who have had conversion or "born-again" experiences may confuse this doorway into faith with faith itself. Being "born-again," while it can be a crucial beginning to our faith journey, is not an end in itself.

Faith is always growing, seeking, and expanding in much the way Jesus describes the kingdom of God when he says, "It is like a mustard seed, which, when sown upon the ground, is the smallest of all the seeds on earth; yet when it is sown it grows up and becomes the greatest of all shrubs, and puts forth large branches, so that the birds of the air can make nests in its shade" (Mark 4:31-32). Faith, like a mustard seed, often begins in our hearts as something tiny that—with proper attention—we can nurture into something great. Our search for God expands our faith.

Like anything that grows, faith requires nurture and care. Whenever we become content or complacent with our faith, it begins to wither. Because the great people of faith throughout the centuries always sought more, their faith grew. No matter how far they had come, they always felt that there was so much further to travel.

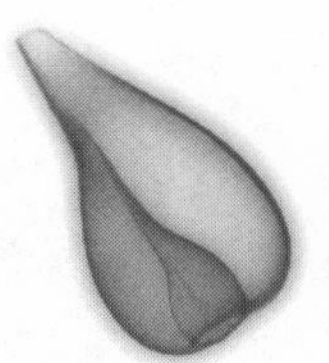

2 We also must remember that *faith always entails balance.* As Christians, we need to be careful that our faith doesn't move to extremes. Christ's way is a balanced way that resists rigid categorization. It is a creative, renewed, and reformed pathway that seeks an open and balanced course. Adopting extreme pathways—pathways that focus only on one or a few aspects of faith while ignoring others—often leads us to replace the one, true God with false gods.

A blind and passive trust in God, in which we refuse to accept responsibility for our actions, is just as detrimental to our spiritual health as a faith that accepts too much personal responsibility for doing God's will. A passive faith turns everything over to God, while an overly responsible faith refuses to turn anything over to God. A faith that emphasizes action without prayer is just as detrimental as one that emphasizes prayer without action. Giving ourselves completely over to a church or community by denying our own uniqueness is as extreme as seeking faith in total isolation from a community. A faith that focuses only on scripture may be as harmful as a faith that refuses to accept the guidance of scripture. Adopting a faith that cares about the poor but detests the wealthy is just as misplaced as a faith that kowtows to the wealthy while ignoring the poor.

Pursuit of balance makes forming a strong faith difficult. As humans, we often gravitate toward extremes of thought, belief, and action. We have trouble holding different or opposing ideas together in tension. For example, how do we balance God's judgment with God's forgiving love? Both are part of God. However, balance does not mean staking a middle ground in everything. Balance connotes a willingness to listen and an openness to all positions of faith, for the Holy Spirit generally speaks through all people—even those we consider extreme. At the same time we have to examine ourselves continually so we can recognize when we have moved too far and need to rebalance our faith in God.

3 We have to recognize that *faith is always relational.* Forming a strong faith begins by rooting ourselves in a relationship with God and then allowing the love of that relationship to flow through us in compassionate relationships with others. Even people who seek to deepen their faith through solitude need this foundation. Those who seek spiritual solitude do not do so out of scorn for the world but out of a need to discipline themselves so they can center themselves primarily in God. This centering allows them to respond more compassionately to others and the world. Solitude is an intensive attempt to forge a stronger relationship between ourselves and God.

Even the most isolated hermits or monks always begin with a tradition and a community; and they remain connected to the community, even though that may mean maintaining a very distant connection. Eventually these hermits and monks return to community, whether that be in life or death. Solitude is temporary; faith always leads to a permanent relationship with God.

4 Maintaining a strong faith despite the gale winds of this world requires that we *anchor our lives in God.* I remember a sermon in which the minister encouraged us to "keep the main thing the main thing." Throughout life, various fads attract our attention, encouraging us to make other things the *main* thing. These fads can be material (fashions, toys, hairstyles), social (lifestyles, hobbies, pursuits); or they can be spiritual. Fads grapple for our attention and demand our obedience. However, growing in faith means focusing on God despite the changing fads.

Maintaining a strong faith despite the gale winds of this world requires that we anchor our lives in God.

Today spirituality has become a fad. In our shower at home, we have a body gel that is aromatic and promises to offer the user "spiritual refreshment." I have yet to receive the supposed spiritual effects of this product. Many *things* of no particular spiritual significance now are advertised as tonics for the body, mind, and spirit. Again, growing spiritually means keeping the main thing the main thing—keeping our focus on God, not fads.

Spirituality becomes a fad when it focuses too much on prayer and meditative techniques, interior experiences, and transformed consciousness while forgetting the purpose of these practices. While these are all part of the true spiritual search, spirituality is primarily about seeking God in all circumstances. These activities help us seek God, but they are not ends in themselves. The fads of spirituality can distract us, pull us away from real spiritual growth. Spiritual growth includes allowing prayer and meditation to help us relate with God on deeper levels. As we grow with God, we often receive gifts of interior insight, peace, and joy. Spiritual growth also may lead to a transformed consciousness. But if we focus on these things as ends in themselves, instead of as means to loving God, they become traps that snare our faith and detour our faith journey.

We live in the midst of a hurricane called life, and it always threatens to blow us off course. The hurricane's winds can confuse us, making us uncertain and frustrating our attempts to forge a more meaningful course in life. It is important that we recognize that the formation of a strong faith requires growing continually, keeping a sense of balance, maintaining a relational focus, and focusing on God. Faith requires that we open our lives to God, that we allow God to be our center, our aim, and our end. Faith assures us of God's blessing.

This book will attempt to help you, the seeker, deepen your faith and grow spiritually by providing a faith foundation so you can weather the winds of life. The focus is not to provide answers to all of your questions but instead to offer a solid foundation upon which you can anchor your faith.

This book emerges from my training and experience as a therapist, as a minister, and as a person like you who struggles with the demands of life. It integrates many of the insights and concepts arising out of the discipline of formative spirituality. This discipline was taught for over thirty years at Duquesne University's Institute of Formative Spirituality. Formative spirituality and its corresponding science, the science of foundational human formation, arose from the vision of Adrian van Kaam. He developed a foundational discipline that integrates insights from spiritual and practical theology, as well as philosophy and the human sciences. Many of the book's insights come out of my five years of study and training in this discipline.

We live in the midst of a hurricane called life, and it always threatens to blow us off course.

One of the treasured spiritual disciplines I learned during my studies at Duquesne University is the discipline of formative reading. This way of reading helps persons form their lives in healthier ways. Our present culture so overwhelms us with information that we have a difficult time reading slowly, reflectively, and meditatively. We read quickly with the intent of gathering, dissecting, and analyzing information. We try to figure out what the point is, and we try to do it quickly so that we can move on to the task of gathering more information. Perhaps the cultural fragmentation and divisiveness of today stems from our inability to integrate what we read. Information for information's sake leads to knowledge, not wisdom; yet God calls us to lives filled with wisdom, not just knowledge. Gathering information gives us knowledge, while reading formatively and reflectively helps us gain the wisdom necessary to live a good life.

When we read something formatively and spiritually, we read it in a way that forms our lives and that opens us to the guidance of God's spirit. Formative reading means reading slowly, reflectively, and prayerfully. When we read something formatively, we willingly halt our reading when we come to something that inspires us, confuses us, or causes us to struggle so we can engage in reflection and prayer.

As a way of helping you, the reader, engage in this same kind of discipline, I have placed three kinds of questions in the margins throughout each chapter. These are *reflective questions* designed to help you think meditatively about what you have read; *scriptural questions* that engage you with the primary source of formative reading—scripture; and *prayerful questions* that call you to pray to God about what you have read. Allow these questions to make your reading more formative as you reflect on your spiritual journey.

I invite you to explore the spiritual journey. As you read, may you uncover and discover ways to deepen your own faith.

When we read something formatively and spiritually, we read it in a way that forms our lives and that opens us to the guidance of God's spirit.

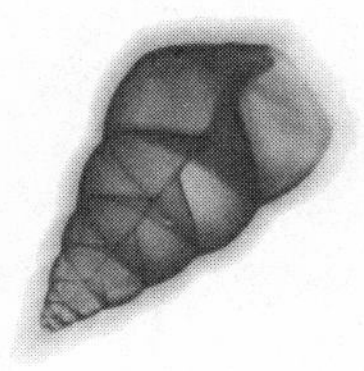

One
Questions of Faith

I STOOD THERE on a hillside looking at the mountains. *This is the place where God wants me to be*, I thought to myself. As a freshman at Roanoke College in Virginia, I could not have affirmed that thought several months earlier. I had planned to go to the University of Virginia but ended up at Roanoke. The folks at the University of Virginia had told me that if I got grades above a certain level at another college, I would be accepted for the second term there. So I stood on a hillside contemplating my choices: *Should I transfer there or stay where I was? Oh Lord, what should I do?* The answer slowly came to me from deep within: *This is the place where God wants me to be.* Something deep within—something connected to God—was saying that God wanted me to be in this place. As I reflect on this experience years later, this "something" proved to be right. Going to Roanoke College turned out to be the best choice I could have made. Had I based my choice on personal ambitions and desires, I might have made another choice. Instead, I based my choice on faith; and it made all the difference.

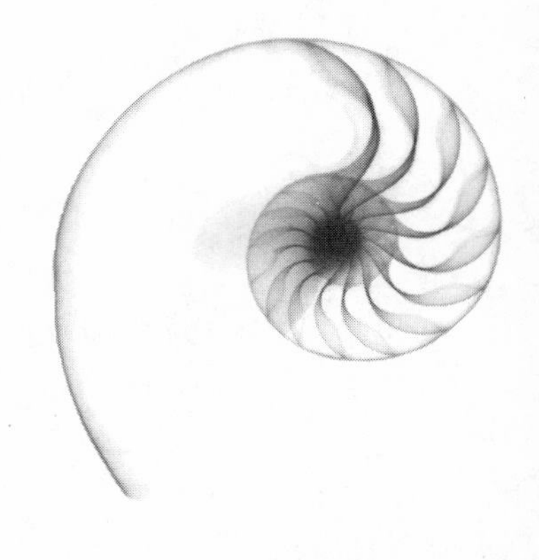

Faith

Faith. What an enigmatic word. The word *faith* conjures up all sorts of images. What does it mean to have faith? We use the word as though we know exactly what it is; yet when we try to describe it, we can't. We can't quite grasp everything faith is. Many wonderful books, essays, and sermons about faith go on and on without giving us a clear understanding. Trying to understand faith raises as many questions as it answers.

How do you define faith?

Take time to reflect on what faith is and what it means to you.

I discovered how hard it is to define faith during a conversation with a struggling teenager. We were discussing the value of going to church or being a Christian. The teenager, a bright and curious young man, lived life in his head. Everything required a rational answer. Religion and God did not make rational sense to him, and he dismissed them as crutches for weak people. I had returned only recently to the church I had rejected many years earlier and was still groping for my own answers. We went back and forth in our discussion, and it turned into a wonderful duel. Each of us tried to make his own points while exposing the other's flaws. Finally I said something that would settle the question once and for all: "Well, you just can't understand anything I'm saying unless you have faith. Otherwise, it makes no sense."

What a confident master stroke on my part! How could he respond to that? His response left me groping for words: "Okay, then just what is faith, if it's so important?" What could I say? I tried to answer, "It's something you just have. It's a belief, but it's also something more. You can't know what faith is unless you have it." I spoke the truth, but it made no rational sense. I did not convince him because I could not articulate the meaning of faith with certainty.

Is Faith a Belief?

My answer failed primarily because I called faith a *belief.* Faith is belief, but what kind of belief? Is it simply a belief that God exists, or a belief in a certain set of theological dogmas? Is it belief in a set of principles or ideas? Is it belief in a religious tradition and its rituals and practices? The problem with calling faith a belief lies in the fact that it is easy to mistake rational belief for transcendent belief. We often mistake rational belief for faith. We base rational belief upon what we logically believe to be true. For example, when we drive down the road we believe that the cars in the approaching lane will remain on their side of the yellow line. If we did not believe this we could never drive anywhere. We would be so afraid that we would never leave home.

The kind of belief that applies to faith is a *spiritual* or *transcendent belief.* This belief goes beyond logic and proof. It goes beyond the level of ordinary belief. Spiritual beliefs are beliefs about spiritual matters that we come to know in our hearts.[1]

Usually faith is built upon something more than logic. For instance, to some extent it made sense for the disciples to believe in Jesus prior to his death on the cross. Jesus performed many fantastic feats and deeds that proved his specialness. In addition, he taught them a coherent theology of love and God's presence that filled them with hope. However, their beliefs were rooted more in logic and proof than they were in spiritual depth. As Jesus said, "Blessed are those who have not seen and yet have come to believe" (John 20:29). With Jesus' death on the cross and with the destruction of the source of their rational belief, the disciples' belief crumbled. They had hoped that Jesus was the messiah, but now he was dead. Perhaps he was just a prophet after all. Even worse, maybe Jesus had been merely a charismatic fool seeking his own glory. They huddled behind locked doors wondering what to do.

Only after the resurrection did the disciples' rational belief become spiritual belief. They formed a faith that moved beyond the rational and known. They developed a belief in something ultimate. Their belief moved beyond mere theology, even though theology helped them understand their growing spiritual belief. Their faith became spiritual as they formed a belief around the core of life. They came to understand that something existed beyond the known, and they learned to cling to this mysterious reality no matter what. This transcendent belief marked the beginning of their real faith. This kind of belief served as the basis of Jesus' words, "Blessed are those who have not seen and yet have come to believe."

Reflect upon your own faith.

In what ways does it depend upon rational beliefs and proof?

How can you form a faith that is more spiritual in nature, more accepting of God's mysterious and ambiguous ways?

Moving beyond Belief

Faith moves beyond rational belief to spiritual belief—to believing with the heart *and* the mind. To believe with our hearts, we have to approach life from a more intuitive, receptive, spiritual, and meditative way of thinking and understanding. Believing with the mind is more rational, analytical, cognitive, and discursive. When we believe with the mind, we accept something because it makes rational and logical sense. When we believe with the heart, we believe because we intuitively and spiritually sense that something is true. It makes sense in our hearts, not just our heads. We do not ignore rational thought, but we integrate it with deeper ways of knowing—with the knowing of the heart.

Spiritual belief relies on the heart's perceptions as well as the

Growing spiritually means becoming more comfortable with uncertainty and ambiguity.

mind's thoughts. Belief—even in its spiritual form—does not tell us completely what faith is. Faith goes beyond even spiritual belief. Having faith means not only believing but also accepting God's mysterious ways rather than clinging to the certainty we normally demand in life. Having faith means *becoming more comfortable with God's mystery.*

Ambiguity and uncertainty create discomfort among many people. A professor of mine once said that growing spiritually does not mean becoming more certain about life. It means becoming more comfortable with uncertainty and ambiguity. Over time, I have come to appreciate this idea deeply. We somehow believe that faith will make things clearer in our minds, but it often doesn't. People with strong faith cannot see the future any more clearly than the rest of us. Nor can they understand present events any better than anyone else. The real difference is that people with a strong faith feel more at ease with life's ambiguities—the grays of life—because they accept life as mystery and acknowledge God's ways as mystery, which are sensed rather than figured out. With a strong faith we can accept God's mystery and purpose instead of demanding that life be painted in black and white.

Reflect upon your life.

In what ways have you been like Paul and followed God despite the uncertainty of what would happen in your life?

The Apostle Paul demonstrates the acceptance of God's mystery instead of demanding certainty. While on a trip to Damascus to persecute Christians, Paul (at the time a Pharisee named Saul) has a blinding vision of Jesus (Acts 9:2-9). Suddenly he becomes painfully aware that his zeal to crush the early Christian movement does not lie within God's will. This vision changes Paul's life, shrouding his previous certainties in uncertainty. Before the vision, he knew with certainty that all followers of the Way were corrupt and blasphemous, but now he does not know what to believe. All he can do is accept Christ's call for him to follow, even though he cannot see the way.

Paul spends the next three years in Arabia (Gal. 1:17-18), studying, reflecting, and growing spiritually. Then he spends another fourteen years deepening his faith (Gal. 2:1) while trying to discern how to follow Christ more deeply. What most people never realize is that Paul does not begin his "official" ministry until seventeen years after his conversion. With the initial vision, Paul does not know where his journey will end; but he follows anyway. Later his ministry always seems to go from one crisis to another as the churches he starts sputter, struggle, bicker, and fight. Failures always temper success.

Along the way Paul suffers constant ridicule, beatings, imprisonment, and the threat of death. Why does he persist in the face of this uncertainty? He persists because in faith he has learned to cling to Jesus' mysterious way even when he does not know where it will lead. Faith means accepting God's mystery over certainty. As Paul said, we see through a glass darkly—we see an obscured vision (1 Cor. 13:12). By living our lives in faith, faith can overcome our dark vision.

Faith then is the spiritual believing of the heart coupled with a faithful acceptance of mystery—of Christ's mysterious and transforming ways. If we leave it at this, faith sounds static and fixed (if we just spiritually believe the right things and accept mystery, then we have faith), as though we can obtain it once and for all. This approach overlooks the fact that faith is dynamic and forming, always in process. We have a hard time defining faith because it is always changing. A child's faith is generally less mature than that of a teenager. A teenager's faith is generally more limited than that of an adult. The qualities of faith of a young adult differ from those of an older person. The faith of a new Christian is perhaps not as deep and well-formed as the faith of a person who has spent many years trying to follow Christ. The more life experiences we have, the more potential these experiences have to form and deepen our faith.

To what extent are your actions rooted in faith?

To what extent does your faith emerge through your actions?

Take time to pray and talk with God about how you can root the different aspects of your daily life more in faith.

The Divine Spark

Ultimately, faith is a *divine spark*—a natural, God-given ability—that burns at the heart of our actions and efforts and that seeks to burn brighter and stronger. Our responsibility comes in providing tinder for the spark so that it can burn more brightly in our lives. In his letter to the Galatians, Paul states that our faith, not our actions, truly matters in life. He emphasizes that faith needs to precede action (Gal. 2:16). Good deeds, unmotivated by by the divine spark of faith, lack the energy to burn long and strong. Good deeds fueled by the spark of faith become God's actions. This does not mean that good deeds lack merit when not founded on faith. It merely means that our faith matters more than our deeds. The power of our actions depends upon the mysterious connection we have with God. If we cut our actions off from God, then they simply become a candle without a flame.

So do our deeds matter, or does just our faith matter? Of

course, our deeds matter. Good deeds strengthen a growing faith. The writer of the epistle of James recognizes the deep connection between faith and action, yet he emphasizes that our actions must incarnate and embody our faith (James 2). While faith ignites action, a faith that does not lead to action is a dead one. In effect, a faith that does not lead to good deeds and daily practice is not really faith; true faith finds expression in daily life.

The inability to connect faith to life is a problem many of us face. We may want to exercise our faith, yet over time we may succumb to life's distractions. When we allow the competing demands of life to constrict our faith, it slowly atrophies from lack of exercise. Thus, while the spark of faith must ignite action, our actions fuel our faith.

Faith requires an abandoning trust, a willingness to give ourselves over to God by giving up our need to control the direction of our lives.

Trust Within

Two essential elements feed the divine spark of faith. Without these, faith smolders and dies. The first element is *trust.* Without a sense of trust, faith becomes nothing more than potential. All people have the potential to form a strong and lasting faith, yet some of us lack the trust to let it grow. What kind of trust do we need? We need an *abandoning trust* instead of the *cautious trust* we have toward God that normally passes for real trust.

Faith requires an *abandoning trust,* a willingness to give ourselves over to God by giving up our need to control the direction of our lives. Relinquishing our need to control life deepens our faith. However, forming an abandoning trust requires that we make a foundational decision.[2] We have to decide whether to trust God completely or to give in to our distrust of God. All of us tend to distrust God to one extent or another. Often this distrust causes us to protect ourselves from God. This protection can take the form of atheism if we deeply distrust God, or agnosticism and indifference to God if we just aren't sure.

While it is one of the most important human characteristics, our ability to trust has been tempered with a kind of learned suspicion. Our disappointment with the people around us, the world, and even God fosters this suspicion. If we did not receive the affection we craved as infants, we will be suspicious of others. If as children we felt neglected, ignored, or even abused, our ability to trust is affected. If family, friends, and acquaintances have rejected us, we can become cautious. If someone we dearly love

dies, that event can leave us feeling alone and fearful—we can learn to distrust life and God. The more we have been disappointed or hurt in life, the less we trust others and God. Thus, we cautiously control our level of trust. We hold back by trusting only those people or things that prove their worthiness. Unfortunately, trying to control our level of trust can also erode our faith.

To foster a deep faith, we not only need to abandon ourselves to God, but we need to do it joyfully. Abandoning ourselves to God becomes joyous when we trust God with a sense of enthusiasm and anticipation. This joyous abandonment reminds me of Peter's response to Jesus when he first sees Jesus after the Resurrection (John 21). Once he recognizes Jesus on the beach, Peter jumps into the water and excitedly swims toward Jesus. Overcome by joy, he abandons himself to Christ. In a sense, this joyous abandonment also reminds me of a dog's waiting for the children to come home from school. The dog jumps, barks, and scratches at the door in joyous anticipation of loving companions. The children enter, and a fury of petting, hugging, and joyous celebration ensues. This kind of joyous abandon lies at the core of a strong and dynamic faith.

When we trust God with joyous abandon, we trust God so deeply that we listen for Christ in every moment of our lives. We trust in God's grace, and we follow Christ no matter where he may lead. We spiritually believe that Christ will take care of us, so we willingly abandon ourselves to God. Paraphrasing the German theologian Dietrich Bonhoeffer, we might say that "only those who believe listen to Christ, and only those who listen to Christ believe."[3] Thus, there is a dynamic relationship between abandoning ourselves to Christ and listening to Christ. The word *abandon* literally means to put ourselves under the proclamation or summons of another. When we abandon ourselves to others, we listen to them and follow their guidance. When we joyously abandon ourselves to God, we listen for God deeply in our hearts, allow God's voice to guide us, and open our hearts to God's grace. So the first element that fuels the divine spark of faith is trust, which originates within us.

Is your faith joyous? Take time to reflect upon your life. What aspects of your life may be more joyful than you acknowledge?

God's Grace

The second element of faith lies completely beyond our control: the element of *God's grace.* We can do only so much to nurture our faith. Without God's grace there can be no true faith. Our need for God's grace is like a seed's attempt to grow. The seed can have all the right genetic packaging and potential, but without the nourishing effects of soil, water, and sun, growth will not occur. God's grace nourishes our faith in a way that we cannot possibly do alone. Unfortunately many people fear this essential aspect of faith. Why? Let us return to a previous discussion for an answer.

Read Matthew 26:36-56.

What kind of trust does Jesus exemplify as he prays?

What kind of faith do the disciples display?

What blocks you in trusting God more fully?

Earlier we discussed the difficulty of developing faith because of our suspicions. We often harbor an especially strong suspicion about God. We wonder, *Does God really care about me? If God really loves me, then why do so many bad things happen? What will happen if I really abandon myself to God?* We have a hard time accepting the fact that God's grace lies completely beyond our control. God has the power to bestow or withhold grace, and this disturbs us. As John Calvin states, "God has always been free to shower... grace on whoever [God] wants to."[4] In other words, we can do all the good deeds we want, but that doesn't mean that God *has* to save or redeem us in response. God's grace is a gift, not a right. This idea makes us uncomfortable. Again we wonder, *What if God chooses to withhold grace? What if I have all the desire in the world to grow in my faith and God decides to ignore me?* For many people, God is scary. We cannot control God, and we certainly cannot control how God chooses to act in our lives.

This inability to control God and God's actions gets at the heart of why so many people seek alternatives to Christian faith. Many of the alternative psychological and spiritual practices offer people a way either to ignore God or to pretend that they have some control over God.

The growth of most cults stems from their offering adherents the illusion of control: As long as adherents read sacred writings the right way, eat certain foods, maintain certain relational practices, and obey their leaders, God will do good things in their lives. Some Christian groups do the same things. They offer a set of rigid beliefs and practices and then blame bad events on a person's failure to maintain these beliefs and practices. They assert that through rigid practice and discipline, God will bless the lives of their members. They forget that it is solely up to God either to bless or curse our lives. We cannot force God to bless, save, or redeem us.

While God is entirely free to bless or curse us, our faith

affirms that God showers grace upon all who seek it. That is our trust. Trust and grace work together to fuel the dynamic spark that burns at the center of an ever-deepening faith. As trusting Christians, we remain open to God's grace, always alert and receptive. Our attitude must be that of a sheep listening for its shepherd. Did you know that each flock of sheep responds only to the sound of its own shepherd? Traditionally among shepherding cultures, the different shepherds gather their sheep together to graze on a mountainside or a field. Five or six flocks of sheep often intermingle and graze together. When the time comes to return home, each shepherd gives a special call and only that shepherd's sheep come running in response. The other sheep continue grazing as though nothing has happened. The sheep listen for and know the sound of their own shepherd. We witness that same response among those who trust in Christ. When we become open to God's grace, then we become sensitive to God's grace; and we rush to accept it.

Look at your life.

What kinds of rigid practices do you follow in an attempt to be independent and self-protecting?

How may they push God away ?

How can you better open yourself to God's grace?

The Shared Journey of Faith

So far, then, faith means growing in *spiritual belief* while also *accepting God's mystery* by letting go of our need for certainty and control. Faith is also a *divine spark* that encourages us to *abandon* ourselves to God and to receive *God's grace.* We need to consider one more aspect of faith: What is the goal of faith? What is its destination and aim?

Faith is a *shared journey toward God,* not just an attempt to get God to act in our lives. In faith we walk along the path, way, or journey to God. Jesus said to his disciples, "I am the way, and the truth, and the life" (John 14:6). As a journey, faith leads to truth and life. Jesus also said, "No one comes to the Father except through me" (John 14:6). Faith is not only a journey; it is a journey that one shares with Jesus—a shared journey, a relationship.

Talk with God right now about how you can listen for Christ more in your life.

Ask how you can learn to trust Christ more in your life.

Listen in silence.

Before entering seminary, I worked as a therapist in a psychiatric hospital. The experience of a particular client reflected how faith is a shared journey with Christ. This client had a manic-depressive disorder, and it was apparent that he would soon move on to a long-term state facility unless he improved drastically in a short period of time. Our sessions had not been going well. One day I walked into his room, and he related a recent experience. A few days before, he had looked out his window and seen Jesus, who showed him a forked path. The right fork went off into the distance and was lined by healthy and successful people. The left fork was lined by addicted, sick, struggling, and hurting people. While acknowledging that the vision was not real, the man believed that it had a message for him. We talked about what it might mean. My client believed that Jesus was telling him that he had to make a choice about his life. The man could take the path leading to a healthy life, or he could stay on his present course and go down a path of increasing difficulty and turmoil. He decided to choose the healthy path. This choice made all the difference because it was a choice that brought healing. Two weeks after this experience, my client returned home rather than moving on to another facility.

Reflect on your life.

When have you faced forks in your life path that required you to decide whether or not to walk the way of health and wholeness?

What choices did you make and why?

Like the client in the hospital, we find ourselves propelled along a journey that entails choice. We constantly face the decision of choosing either the pathways that lead to God or those that lead elsewhere. In this decision making, we encounter real freedom. While the genetic packaging of our bodies, the conditioning of our personal histories, and the restraints of our surroundings constrain us to some extent, we still ultimately have the freedom either to reject or embrace God. While we lack the ability to change much about ourselves and our situations, we do have the freedom to seek God and to seek the journey toward God.

Many of us learn what it means to choose God only in the midst of suffering, oppression, and crisis. Terry Anderson learned this truth when he was held hostage in Lebanon for seven years. During that time, his suffering forced him to face himself and his life. Prior to his capture, he had ignored God by chasing his own ambitions and pleasures. Ironically, his imprisonment freed him to choose the path of faith that leads to God. Recalling his crisis, Anderson says that in his helplessness he finally said to God,

> I can't do this, God. I'm finished. I surrender. There's nothing I can do to change anything, nothing anyone can do. And it's just going to go on, and I can't do it. Help me. There's no reason why you should. Don't we always turn to you when we're in trouble, and away from you when things are good? I'm doing the same. But you say you love me. So help me.[5]

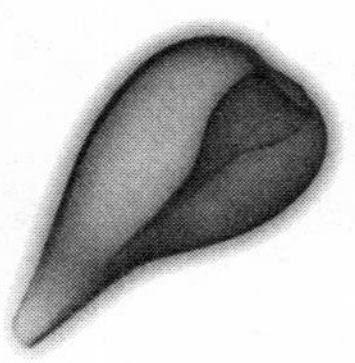

Slowly over time, Anderson sensed a response: "But at the bottom, in surrender so complete there is no coherent thought, no real pain, no feeling, just exhaustion, just waiting, there is something else. Warmth/light/softness."[6]

Like Terry Anderson, we have a constant yearning to journey toward God, yet often it takes a crisis to set us on the path. Too often we let the desires of our bodies, the pains of our past, or our fears of the future determine how we will live.

While faith is a journey, it is always a shared journey with Christ. Even when we choose to reject or avoid God and the pathways of faith, I am convinced that Jesus still shares our journey. Jesus simply waits for those moments when we are willing to notice him. It took being held against his will for Terry Anderson to notice Christ. It took mental illness and psychiatric hospitalization for my client to recognize Christ. It need not take all these extremes for us though. At any moment, we can choose to recognize Christ who shares our journey. At any moment, we can choose to walk along the journey with Christ as we move toward God.

What parts of your life keep you from choosing God's pathways?

Take time to talk with God about this, and then listen for God's response in silence. Listen with your heart.

The Journey of Love

Faith is a shared journey toward God; and above all, it is a journey of love. One central theme grounds all Christian faith: love. The journey of faith is a shared journey that deepens our love for God. Luke's Gospel makes this plain. Jesus asserts that the key to life emerges from one rule: "You shall love the Lord your God with all your heart, and with all your soul, and with all your strength, and with all your mind; and your neighbor as yourself" (Luke 10:27).

Faith is a shared journey toward God; and above all, it is a journey of love.

I find it fascinating how often we focus on the second part of this passage and forget the first. When teaching, I often ask people what this passage says. Most reply that it says we need to love one another. This response reveals how easily we push ourselves away from God. When we look at the passage more deeply, it reveals that even before we can love others, we should love God with all our mind, heart, soul, and strength. Faith, then, is primarily the journey of continually deepening our love for God.

If we try to love others through obedience to scripture or tradition, we find that these serve as poor substitutes for God. We forget that theology, scripture, religion, tradition, ritual, and community exist to deepen our love for God—to deepen our relationship with God. When obedience to these things becomes more important than our love for God, then they get in our way.

Do not misunderstand me. A popular fad of our time makes fun of theology, scripture, religion, tradition, ritual, and community. People say these things get in the way of spirituality. Yet theology and religious practices, when properly balanced, help us fall in love with God. They only become a problem when we make them idols—substitutes for God.

How do you deepen your love for God?

Pray about this and ask God to lead you to a deeper love.

Those who reject all of these practices and cling to the false belief that they can find God alone face an even larger problem. The pursuit of God in isolation from others becomes a false idol because it makes our own whims the only true route to God. In our desire to control our own journeys, we reject the wisdom and guidance of all these traditions and pathways so that we can egotistically and selfishly make our own visions the dominant ones. Seeking God without the help of theology, church, rituals, and community means ignoring the fact that the nurturing love of God comes through the guidance and love of others.

Faith is, above all, a journey of love. Like all love relationships, it has peaks and valleys, joys and sorrows, periods of peace and turmoil. Falling in love with anyone means encountering all sorts of ups and downs, for it entails the merging of desires, hopes, and visions, an uneven process at best. The ups and downs of falling in love with God are similar. As we grow more deeply in love with God, as we share our lives with God—we merge our hopes and aspirations with God's hopes and aspirations. Thus, the journey of faith is a journey in which Jesus nurtures us as we fall in love with him, and in doing so he shares with us the adventures along this journey.

Forming our faith means nurturing spiritual beliefs while simultaneously learning to accept God's mystery over our need for certainty. We nourish faith's divine spark by abandoning ourselves to God in trust while opening ourselves to God's grace. In this way we allow our growing faith to invigorate the actions of our lives. Fostering our growing faith means choosing to walk along the journey of faith with Christ toward God. Finally, walking along this journey of faith encourages our deepening love affair with God who is our source and our aim, our life and our love.

Two
Expectations

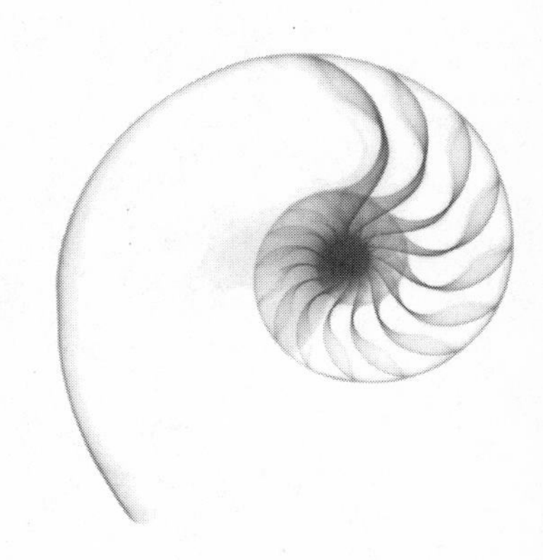

IN THE PREVIOUS chapter we talked about faith as a journey—a journey that leads us to fall more and more deeply in love with God. Falling in love with God is actually the whole point of our spiritual journey. When we try to turn the faith journey into something else, such as a search for insight or bliss, our spiritual growth is stunted. Faith is about love, and everything else that comes as a result of faith is by-product, not purpose. The call to love God with all our mind, heart, and soul serves as the guiding light that shines ahead of us as we walk along the faith journey.

We use a wonderful metaphor when we call the process of deepening our faith a "journey." The term *journey* clearly demonstrates the fact that faith is more than just a state or quality that we develop and form. Faith is a yearning that beckons and urges us to come and live with God. It is a directed, lifelong desire for God that we cannot control or plan. Forming a deep faith means intentionally choosing to jump into the current or flow of grace that runs through life. Like a sailing ship exploring new lands, faith is a vessel that yearns to flow with the current of God's grace while simultaneously catching the winds of God's spirit. One of the struggles of the faith journey is that, like a ship exploring new lands, we never know what to expect.

Expectations

As spiritual explorers, we often *expect* certain things to happen when we take the faith journey seriously. When we follow God and discover that God is leading us in wholly unexpected life directions, we get confused. We often carry unrealistic and misleading expectations of what will happen if we commit our lives to the currents of God's grace. Some people think that growing spiritually means never having to struggle in life again. Others believe it involves the development of special insights and powers. Unrealistic expectations can cause problems when the demands of the faith journey clash with our fantasies, leaving us feeling frustrated, lost, and disappointed. Eventually this disappointment can erode our faith. So it is important to remember that walking along the journey of faith means maintaining realistic expectations of what lies ahead. True faith entails a willingness to follow Christ's path instead of the pathways of our own desires.

Let me offer an example through an ancient story. A spiritual master reflected on his life in old age, and he thought to himself,

> "I was a revolutionary when I
> was young and all my prayer to God was
> 'Lord, give me the energy to change
> the world.'
>
> As I approached middle age and realized
> that half my life was gone without my
> changing a single soul, I changed my
> prayer to 'Lord, give me the grace to change
> all those who come in contact
> with me. Just my family and friends,
> and I shall be satisfied.'
>
> Now that I am an old man and my days
> are numbered, my one prayer
> is, 'Lord, give me the grace to change
> myself.' If I had prayed for this right
> from the start I should not have wasted
> my life."[1]

What have been your expectations with regard to serving God and the impact that service would have on your life and the lives of others?

What events have disappointed you?

What events have surprised you?

Take time to reflect on these questions.

We often spend our lives pursuing misguided desires, ambitions, and expectations. Like the spiritual master, we can waste our lives in stubborn pursuit of these misdirected expectations. Let us look at certain expectations of the journey that we should maintain as we attempt to deepen our loving faith. When we keep these expectations in our hearts, they engender a freshness and purpose in our faith that deepens and invigorates our lives.

Expect the Unexpected

Every summer while I was between the ages of ten and thirteen, my parents sent me to a camp in New Hampshire for eight weeks. Over the course of the summer, we campers hiked various New Hampshire mountains. My experiences in those mountains paralleled the experiences we face as we journey through the mountains of faith. I discovered that sometimes the trails are more difficult and longer than we expect. Other times, when the trails seem as though they will go on forever, they suddenly end at unforeseen summits. Sometimes trails run beside streams of incredible beauty, while other times they slog through mud and marshes teeming with mosquitoes and horseflies. Whatever happens along the way, it is rarely what we expect.

Reflect on your life.

How has it changed over time?

How did you expect it to turn out?

How does your life differ from your expectations?

The faith journey is the same kind of experience. We can expect the journey of faith—the spiritual journey—to lead to unexpected places and to bring unexpected changes to our lives. These changes can be both exhilarating and disturbing. The one constant in our spiritual growth is that we will change and be transformed in ways we do not expect. It can be no other way because growing in Christ means continual transformation and renewal. The Apostle Paul understood this and expressed it by saying, "Do not be conformed to this world, but be transformed by the renewing of your minds, so that you may discern what is the will of God—what is good and acceptable and perfect" (Rom. 12:2). Paul recognized that becoming more sensitive to God's will in our lives requires continual reappraisal and renewal of how we view life, the world, and ourselves. We have to be willing to go where we normally would not choose to go. We have to be willing to let God change our lives.

The story of the Hebrew exodus from Egypt to the Promised Land serves as a classic example of how God transforms us. The Hebrew people wanted to reach the Promised Land quickly, but they were not yet prepared. Their weak faith made them easy prey for distractions. They needed to be transformed into a people with a strong and responsible faith before they could embrace God's purpose for them. Over forty years God led them on a journey of transformation. So too in our personal journeys, God leads us on a journey of transformation. God's journey requires patience and perseverance as God transforms our hearts, minds, and souls.

However, we do not accept this process of transformation easily. The process of being transformed and renewed in all aspects of our lives often creates a sense of turmoil and crisis. We face turning points that demand decision. To make it through these crises, we have to ask questions deep within our hearts: *Am I seeking God's way or my own? Am I willing to follow God's path even if it leads me along a difficult and scary course, or will I fearfully try to cling to the way of life that is passing away?* Our response to these critical questions determines whether or not we will conform our lives to God's purpose.

Think about the major crises of your life.

Did you try to keep things as they were, or were you willing to change your life?

How open to God's spirit were you during these times?

Adrian van Kaam says that each life crisis has a deeper *transcendence crisis* at its core. At these times we receive the opportunity to move from a lower to a higher form of spiritual life.[2] Every life crisis thrusts a transcendent or spiritual decision upon us: *Am I willing to transcend or go beyond the constraints of my normal ways of living? Am I willing to change my life for God, or am I going to keep following the world's way?* Life experiences become spiritual crises when we try to hold fast to our present way of life in the face of situations that demand transformation and renewal.

When I think about expectations, crises, and transformation, my thoughts turn to the Apostle Peter. Jesus' arrest generates a spiritual crisis within Peter: Should he admit that he is a follower of Jesus, or should he protect himself and hide? Peter had expected a reward for his faith, not persecution. He expected that following Jesus would lead to glory, not this unexpected turn into darkness. With Jesus' arrest, Peter chooses to protect himself. He conforms his mind to the fears of the world by denying his faith in Jesus.

By denying Jesus, Peter avoids transforming his life. He avoids the unexpected journey. Peter's life does change when Jesus gives Peter a chance to redeem himself. At the end of John's Gospel, Jesus asks Peter three times, "Simon, son of John, do you love me?" (John 21). Each question corresponds to one of Peter's previous denials of Jesus. Three times Peter replies, "You know that I love you." Then Jesus says to him, "Very truly, I tell you, when you were younger, you used to fasten your own belt and to go wherever you wished. But when you grow old, you will stretch out your hands, and someone else will fasten a belt around you and take you where you do not wish to go" (John 21:17-18). Jesus is telling Peter that if he follows him, the journey will not lead to safety. Despite this warning, Peter makes a commitment. He accepts the unexpected journey, even in the face of Jesus' prediction that the journey will lead to Peter's imprisonment and death. Peter chooses to follow Jesus along the unexpected journey of faith, and it makes all the difference in his life.

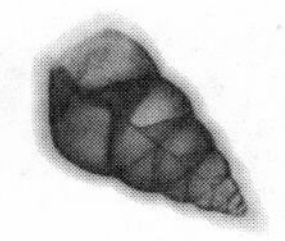

We have that same choice. Christ calls us to follow in an unexpected journey of faith. Where it leads only God knows. We must decide whether to follow in faith or hide in fear.

Expect Valleys and Deserts

In her wonderful allegory, *Hinds' Feet on High Places,* Hannah Hurnard illustrates one of the toughest struggles we face if we choose to follow Christ. She points out how unprepared most of us are for the difficulties that lie on our journey toward God. Her title character Much-Afraid (who represents our own fears) helps us discover how ill-prepared we are. Much-Afraid wants to follow the Great Shepherd (Christ), but she fears the path he tells her to follow. As she travels along the Shepherd's path, she complains constantly. She wants to follow the Shepherd along an easy path, not the one that leads through valleys, deserts, pain, loneliness, and turmoil. She resists the path that the Shepherd sets for her, and she really resists the sorrow and suffering that accompany her along the way.[3]

We all want our personal journeys to be ones of continual bliss and pleasure, yet we forget that the point of the journey is to fall in love with God.

Hurnard shows us that while the journey of faith moves continually towards God's kingdom, it often includes long stretches of spiritual desert and darkness. We don't want to hear this. We don't like these periods of confusion, especially if they cause us to feel pain, uncertainty, and difficulty. So we say we want to follow God's way, but at the same time we resist it. Much-Afraid clearly demonstrates this resistance as she pleads with the Shepherd to change the path he has set for her:

> "Shepherd," [Much-Afraid] said despairingly, "I can't understand this. The guides you gave me say that we must go down there into that desert, turning right away from the High Places altogether. You don't mean that, do you? You can't contradict yourself. Tell them we are not to go there, and show us another way. Make a way for us, Shepherd, as you promised."

> He looked at her and answered very gently, "That is the path, Much-Afraid, and you are to go down there."
>
> "Oh, no," she cried. "You can't mean it. You said if I would trust you, you would bring me to the High Places, and that path leads right away from them. It contradicts all that you promised."
>
> "No," said the Shepherd, "it is not contradiction, only postponement for the best to become possible."[4]

Much-Afraid shows us how much we all fear the faith journey because it does not meet our expectations. As would we, Much-Afraid wants to travel to the High Places—the places of spiritual maturity and peace—but she wants a painless and happy journey. We all want our personal journeys to be ones of continual bliss and pleasure, yet we forget that the point of the journey is to fall in love with God. That requires transformation at the deepest levels of our being. We have to become conformed to God's will, which means allowing our will to be transformed so that we can serve God's call instead of our own desires and ambitions. The process of transformation sometimes leads us into confusing and lonely deserts, misty and deep valleys of uncertainty, muddy and ambiguous bogs that seem to have no end. When we trust God, all of these can become places in which our faith deepens and grows stronger.

Have you gone through experiences in which it seemed that you were being led into a desert?

How did you respond?

Talk with God about how you want to respond to these situations in the future.

God's interest in our transformation serves as the impetus for Jesus' going out into the desert prior to his ministry (Matt. 4:1-7). In ancient Judaism and Christianity, the desert represented a place where people learned to trust God with their lives, a place that developed people's awareness of their fragility, weakness, and helplessness. The trying conditions of the desert taught them to trust and depend upon God.

Read 2 Corinthians 12:1-10, which describes how turmoil and difficulty can lead to a deeper faith.

What does it mean to you when God says, "My grace is sufficient for you, for power is made perfect in weakness"?

We don't have to travel to actual deserts to learn these same lessons. Plenty of desert experiences fill our lives, experiences that cause us to feel alone, helpless, forgotten, and thirsty for any sign of hope. Susan Muto says that each personal desert "reminds us that we belong to [God]. It mocks any illusion that we can rely ultimately on ourselves.... What the Lord offers is an admittedly frightening program of ego stripping, but this wounding is a prescription for more personal wholeness."[5] Human deserts can be as dramatic as unjust discrimination, death of a close friend, suffering from illness, sudden unemployment, divorce, or even retirement. They also can be as subtle as a sense of dissatisfaction or unhappiness with present circumstances, uncertainty about the future, and vague discouragement with life. All of these events can place us in a spiritual desert, valley, or bog.

The key to surviving spiritual deserts lies in our acknowledging and affirming the spiritual opportunities our deserts afford us. While painful, our deserts also help reform our lives. This reformation process has three phases.

1 First, since we are often overattached to certain unhealthy lifestyles and practices, our personal deserts may provide opportunities to *let go* of these habits and obsessions that push God out of our lives. The harshness of our deserts encourages us to free ourselves of the things that have been harming our lives. As Carolyn Gratton points out, to awaken our hearts truly, we must let something go.[6] This letting go is a difficult step because we have to let go of "stuff" that has made us feel safe. Yet we have to let it go because it has kept us from God. Letting go of an old, destructive way of living is not easy since old ways are known, and even the best new ways of living are unknown. Every alcoholic faces this crisis: *What will life without drinking be like? How can I live without my beer, my wine, my vodka?* We all face a crisis of leaving the known to move into the unknown whenever life changes. To grow spiritually and to deepen our faith, we have to let go of the selfish, obsessive, or destructive things we do that disconnect God from our lives.

Think of a crisis you faced at some point in your life.

Did it lead to changes in your life?

What did you have to let go of in order to enable that change?

2 The second phase of the faith journey is the struggling phase. We need to *struggle through* periods of conversion and transformation that accompany our movement toward new life. This phase becomes problematic for many of us, especially when our struggle involves an addiction, a divorce, or a new career. While we may want to relinquish a destructive habit, relationship, or lifestyle and become new and different people, we resist the changes taking place. How often have we vowed to change our ways, only to return to old ways of behaving or relating? We return because we cannot handle the struggle with newness. While we hate our old ways, we cannot deal with the pain that accompanies our transition to adopting a new way of living. We cannot deal with the valleys that accompany our journey to a new life.

When you struggled to adopt a new way of life, what was it like?

What new way of life have you embraced?

How well did you adopt it at first?

3 Even as we struggle to release the old life, we need to *embrace* new ways of living with God that foster our spiritual growth.

We may hate our old ways, but we still have a difficult time adopting the new ways. Troubling questions make us stumble. For example, after a divorce, at what point do I start dating? If I find a new mate, how can I be sure I can trust him or her? What if my heart gets broken again?

We can struggle in limbo for years because we never embrace these new ways of living. However, to grow in faith we willingly have to embrace God's ways and God's spirit as it leads us out of our deserts and back to the High Places of God's kingdom.

As we journey through the mountains of faith, we can expect to travel through valleys, deserts, and bogs. The journey requires a willingness to *let go* of destructive ways of living, to *struggle through* the pain of changing our lives, and to *embrace* new ways of living that produce healthier lives. When we recognize the inherent faith struggles, we can balance our spiritual formation in a way that keeps us moving forward no matter what may obscure our way.

Expect Peaks and Wonders

Many Christians view both the faith journey and the life journey as a long string of struggle, disappointment, and pain.

One of the most frightening experiences I had as a youngster in New Hampshire occurred when we campers climbed Mount Bond. In the middle of a four-day hike through the Pemigewassett Wilderness area, we began our ascent on a beautifully clear day. As we neared the top of Mount Bond, a dense fog descended upon us. By the time we reached the summit, the fog enveloped us and seemed to seep all the way into our hearts. As we walked in single file along the trail, we could barely see more than ten feet in any direction. I was scared. If I lost sight of the person in front of me, I might be lost forever on that misty mountain. Fortunately, our guides found the way across the rocky summit by using their compasses, and soon we headed down the other side.

Eventually we made it to our campsite, which was shrouded in mist also. The fog hid everything except the trees in our immediate area. For all I knew, beyond the mist lay a cliff, a bear, or some other unknown danger. My imagination ran wild. That night I had a fitful sleep as I worried about rolling off the wooden platform that served as our mattress, down the mountain, and never being found. When we awoke the next morning, we emerged from our tents to a dazzling sight. The sun shone in a brilliant blue sky, and we could see the stunning mountains that surrounded us—an incredible sight and so unexpected. I had expected only the worst: no view, no sun, no exhilaration—only more fog. Why would I have expected more? Our difficult journey prepared me to expect more of the same. I was very disappointed when we had to leave this surprising view. I wanted to remain in that spot for the rest of my life—or at least until lunch.

The valleys, deserts, and difficulties of the journey can easily discourage us, and we lose hope for the peaks and wonders of the faith journey. Many Christians view both the faith journey and the life journey as a long string of struggle, disappointment, and pain. Over time, they become cynical about life events. They perceive faith as a process of serving an aloof, uncaring, and demanding God. These folks slog through life trying to do the right thing, not because they feel a tremendous calling to do so, but because they do not want to upset God. (I suppose this follows the wisdom of letting sleeping gods lie.) They experience little joy in their faith, only duty and perseverance. Their cynicism can be detected in their relationships with others. Although they may serve on church boards and committees, give money to the church, attend worship weekly, and even pray, they have no real love for others. For them, Christianity is a code of ethics and morals that lacks a sense of vitality and life.

What is your approach to life?

Are you pessimistic, cynical, and doubtful; or are you optimistic, hopeful, and thankful?

Take time to thank God for the wonders and surprises in your life.

Yet Christ calls us to a joyful faith. The joyless faith of duty goes against Christ's call to love the Lord our God with all our heart, mind, soul, and strength. It also goes against the sense of hope that functions as a central part of Christian faith. The writer of First Peter recognized the importance of hope and urged each person to "set all your hope on the grace that Jesus Christ will bring you" (1 Pet. 1:13). Paul also recognized the importance of hope. In his first letter to the Corinthians, Paul acknowledges that faith and love intertwine with a deep sense of hope: "And now faith, hope, and love abide, these three..." (1 Cor. 13:13). Our faith expresses itself in acts of love as well as in our sense of hope. When we undertake the journey of faith, we can expect to encounter peaks and wonders. This is our hope and our faith.

To discover peaks and wonders, we have to stop taking them for granted. On the faith journey we often let life's demands distract us. We go through life focusing so much energy on our jobs, relationships, tasks, and accomplishments (or lack of accomplishments) that we fail to notice the wonders of life. We struggle with wanting God to do so much for us that we cannot see what

God has already done or is doing for us. David Steindl-Rast suggests that our tendency to take things for granted keeps us from waking up to life and to God. He also suggests that God acts *continually* in life to surprise us through the world around us. We recognize it only when we wake up to it: "Our eyes are opened to that surprise character of the world around us the moment we wake up from taking things for granted."[7]

What might make you more hopeful?

Take time in prayer to talk with God about this.

Taking things for granted is a real problem. On the hike through the fog on Mount Bond, I took for granted that nothing good could come from that trip. I felt sure that everything would remain foggy and obscured. That is why the incredible view the next morning shocked me so much. God surprised me when I least expected it. This seems to be one of the ways God works. Even in the midst of despair, God can surprise us with grace.

We can recognize God's grace more clearly by cultivating a sense of *wonder*. Wonder is a childlike openness to life that we often let go of as adults. In fact, we often substitute *curiosity* for wonder.[8] In our curiosity, we literally want to bring an object under the control of our understanding. When we sit in wonder, we marvel in surprise at an object's depth, intricacy, and mystery like a child gazing at a leaf, a bug, the stars, or even food.

Jesus recognized the need for childlike wonder. He stated, "Truly I tell you, unless you change and become like children, you will never enter the kingdom of heaven. Whoever becomes humble like this child is the greatest in the kingdom of heaven" (Matt. 18:3-4). Have you ever watched a little child play? Sometimes children take things apart, but often children are caught in wonder by things—particularly small children. They do not grab things in curiosity in order to figure them out. Instead, they approach things in wonder in order to sense them. Infants touch the objects that come into their world. They smell them, look at them, and suck on them in order to sense what they are. Watch how a child gazes in wonder at something new and different. This is the way God calls us to be with life. We recognize God's grace when we approach life with a sense of wonder—when we allow life to surprise us with peaks and wonders.

How often do you look around in wonder?

How often do you recognize God's surprises?

Look at your hand and try to sense God's grace in it.

Look around you. What else in your life is wonder-full and surprising?

An amazing thing happens to us when we approach life in this way. We wake up to the surprises God has for us. I believe God waits around every corner of our lives, waiting to surprise us. Sometimes in our hurry to move on to the next appointment, we don't even notice God's gift. Sometimes we accept the gift; but in our hurry to move on to something else, we fail to appreciate it. Sometimes we initially accept the gift; but we want something else, and so we reject God's gift. Steindl-Rast recognizes that all of these approaches illustrate how we take God's blessing for granted, and he responds by saying, "Even the predictable turns into surprise the moment we stop taking it for granted."[9]

To grow in our faith, we have to expect God's gifts of grace even in life's darkest moments.

To grow in our faith, we have to expect God's gifts of grace even in life's darkest moments. These gifts of grace surround us. When we take God and God's grace for granted, we get mired in a purely human perspective. When we expect peaks and wonders, we connect with the Divine. Like the perspective we gain of the view from a high mountain summit, recognizing God's grace in our lives helps us take on God's divine perspective—if only for a moment. When we look for and accept God's grace, we allow ourselves to recognize how God acts in our lives.

Expect to Share the Journey

After graduating from college, I spent a week in New Hampshire revisiting the mountains I had hiked in my youth. I really wanted to climb Mount Nancy. As a child, a pond near its summit fascinated me. The pond emptied out into a creek that cascaded down the mountain. When I was twelve, something about that pond and its creek had seemed magical to me. I wanted to rediscover its charm. I had not hiked a mountain in over ten years. When I had, I had hiked as part of a group. Determined to be a self-sufficient hiker and guide on my climb up Mount Nancy, I armed myself with the *Appalachian Mountain Guide* and set out with a friend. We never made it to the top. We kept losing the trail along the way. The guidebook map clearly indicated the trail's moving to the right side of a large creek, but our trail ended in a thorn patch. No matter how hard we tried, we could not find our way.

Dejected, we returned home without ever reaching the top, without ever seeing the magical pond. Several days later, my friend discovered that we had been following the wrong map. In my zeal to take charge of the journey and to climb this mountain without a guide, I had been following the wrong path. The same thing happens to us when we independently seek spiritual growth in isolation from others.

One characteristic of our population today—especially the

How open are you to sharing your journey with others?

Do you tend to see faith as private and personal, or do you tend to see it as something to be shared?

Read Matthew 18:20.

What does this scripture say about sharing our faith?

baby-boom generation and Generation Xers—is the desire to grow spiritually while remaining independent of institutional structures, such as the church, that promote spirituality. Wade Clark Roof, a sociologist of religion, says that members of the baby-boom generation avoid making commitments to any kind of institution, especially religious institutions. He states, "Commitment is a problem in the sense that boomers tend to be fearful and suspicious generally—not just toward religion, but with regard to social attachments as a whole."[10] Having been disillusioned by the Kennedy and King assassinations, the civil rights conflicts, the Vietnam War, the oil crisis, and the national leadership crisis known as Watergate, baby boomers are wary of making commitments that might disillusion them. Thus, they commit to churches or spiritual communities cautiously. Deep down, they fear that they will be disappointed or led astray, so they try to control their own spiritual growth.

This attitude of independent control can lead to *spiritual individualism.* Spiritual individualism supports the belief that persons grow best spiritually by avoiding the contamination of a religious tradition. This belief arises not only from the baby-boom distrust of religion but also from our own American character. Americans tend to be very individualistic,[11] and this individualism can distort our faith and stunt its growth. When we become overly individualistic in terms of our spiritual journey, we can lead ourselves in directions that either go nowhere or lead to false summits.

Those of us pursuing the journey of faith not only need to share the journey with others, but we need to follow adept guides. Spiritual growth emerges from relationships with real people, not just with books, television programs, and personal meditation. When we walk with others along the journey, we support one another as we walk toward God. Our spiritual friendships and guidance assist us in our journey. We connect more solidly with the Holy Spirit. Carolyn Gratton says that spiritual guides and faith friends help us focus on our life direction, pay more attention to our feelings and the distorting habits of our minds and hearts, and recognize the ways we may be blocking the healthy flow of energy in our lives. The faith guide helps us listen more intently for God's call in our lives.[12] In our zeal to forge our own pathways, we often ignore the shared aspect of the faith journey. In so doing, we erode our faith and inhibit spiritual growth.

Thus, to deepen our faith, we need a willingness to share our journey—not only with those seeking spiritual growth but with those willing to help us listen to God. The more we share our journey with others, the more dynamic and satisfying our journey.

Expect to Struggle with Tradition

Our culture traditionally idealizes persons who seek God on their own, especially if they have rejected their own religion or religious roots. Many of the popular spiritual gurus of our age are those who proudly point to the fact that they *were* nuns, monks, priests, or pastors for years—but now have struck out on their own. Somehow, rejecting their religious moorings makes spiritual writers seem so much more qualified. Sometimes we distrust religion and religious traditions so much that we cut ourselves off from the very thing that exists to nurture spiritual growth and the faith journey. As a result, many spiritual seekers take a smorgasbord approach to faith. They pick and choose among different religious beliefs and try to create their own approach. They reject any one tradition and choose to forge their own.

If we are to grow and deepen our faith, then we have to be willing to struggle with our own Christian traditions.

A smorgasbord or buffet approach to faith is tempting. Whenever I go to a Sunday brunch buffet, I rarely eat the really nourishing food. Instead, I look for the sweet and sugary stuff. First, I have a specially made cheese-and-mushroom omelet. Then I go back for some freshly made Belgian waffles and syrup. Next I search for croissants and sweet rolls. Finally, I begin my assault on the cookies, cheesecakes, and anything chocolate. By the time I finish eating, I am stuffed to the gills with great-tasting food that has done nothing for me except expand my waistline. The food tastes great, but it does not nourish. Many people treat faith like a Sunday brunch. Much of the spiritual material that fills the shelves of the local bookstore are morsels that appeal to those searching for spiritual sugar. While these books and tapes fascinate and excite, they provide little spiritual nourishment.

Many of today's spiritual writings draw on a myriad of sources, but few immerse themselves in strong faith traditions. Often writers draw concepts from legitimate and illegitimate traditions and lump them together into a buffet spirituality. In essence, all of these spiritualists take what tastes good and leave behind the stuff that is not as tasty but often more nourishing.

If we are to grow and deepen our faith, then we have to be

willing to struggle with our own Christian traditions. We have to expect to immerse ourselves *in* a religious tradition while struggling *against* it. Both our adherence to and our struggle against a faith tradition can nourish our faith.

In March 24, 1980, Oscar Romero, the archbishop of San Salvador, was assassinated by right-wing militants while celebrating Mass in San Salvador. He had served as archbishop for three years, and during that time he struggled tremendously with his faith. What was God really calling him to do? The Roman Catholic tradition, which advocates obedience to the church, devotion to Christ, rejection of evil, love for all, respect for the dignity and freedom of all people, and compassion for the poor had nurtured him. However, as archbishop, he found himself in the midst of conflict between the need to care for all people and the call to advocate for the poor. Over time, his consciousness rose regarding the government of El Salvador and its brutal torture and murder of left-wing rebels and those suspected of helping them. The church's failure to speak out against this violence also concerned him.

Romero was in a quandary. He wanted to be obedient to the church and stay above these political matters, yet he also felt called to be an advocate for those who had become military targets. Romero wanted to love all people, yet the evils he witnessed in his country's government and in his own church repulsed him. Ultimately, Oscar Romero had to struggle with his religious tradition. His struggle helped him deepen his faith so that he could listen more clearly to Christ.

What things do you struggle with in your own tradition?

How do you stay within your tradition while struggling with certain elements of it?

Romero could have chosen to take an easy route by following the common wisdom of "don't make waves," or he could have left the church. By struggling with and against his religious tradition, he learned to follow Christ more deeply. Eventually his struggles helped him discern Christ's call more clearly. He spoke out against the brutality and called upon the government to accept responsibility for its culpability, an unpopular stand among the other bishops and among the powerful in government. While celebrating Mass, the people he struggled against shot and killed Romero. In his death he became a beacon of hope to people everywhere. Oscar Romero paid the price for following the call of faith, but the matter of ultimate importance was that he acted out of faith, not fear—faith that was deepened in his struggle with his religious tradition.

For all of us, the faith journey requires a struggle with our own religious traditions. This struggle deepens our faith. What are traditions? They are guidelines for living that one generation hands down to the next.[13] Religious traditions teach us how to live with God in the midst of a world that threatens to pull us away from God. Yet over time even the best traditions become infused with ideas and practices that can alter the original calling of these traditions. While response to particular life problems during certain historical periods forms religious traditions, over time other demands arise that ask us to stretch our traditions to meet new challenges.

What is your relationship with your own religious tradition?

Take time to consider what the role of a religious or spiritual tradition should be in your own life?

How do you respond to the difficulties in your life?

Talk with God about how you can respond to life in ways that make your faith stronger.

My own tradition, the Presbyterian tradition, emerged out of the Reformed and Protestant struggle against the church of the sixteenth century that had become overly dogmatic and corrupt. John Calvin and others tried to form a Christian spiritual tradition that, among other things, emphasized the importance of striking a balance between one's Spirit-led individual conscience and one's commitment to the community of Christ. In recent years, this tradition has been stretched as one group within the Presbyterian tradition seeks to emphasize individual conscience and expression regardless of its impact on the community. The other side attempts to form a rigid, dogmatic communal structure regardless of how it inhibits individual conscience and expression. Neither side really grapples with the full meaning of this reformed Christian tradition that emphasizes both the individual and the community. Being nourished by a particular tradition means grappling with all sides, and all faith traditions join in this ongoing struggle.

Struggling with the spiritual, moral, ethical, and doctrinal guidelines of a tradition lets the nourishing power of the tradition sink into our hearts.

To wrestle with any religious tradition, we immerse ourselves deeply in that tradition, allowing its wisdom and guidance to nurture us. If we stay on the surface of a tradition, or worse, stay on the surface of *many* traditions, then we never really let our roots sink down to find good soil and fresh water. Contending with the teachings of a faith tradition is crucial for individuals seeking to deepen their faith. Equally crucial is each particular tradition's struggle with the greater Christian tradition. For instance, the Presbyterian, as well as the Methodist, Baptist, Roman Catholic, Eastern Orthodox, Coptic, and other such denominational traditions, have to wrestle continually with the deeper Christian traditions. They have to grapple with the original calling and teachings of scripture and the church's history. As a matter of fact, the entire Christian tradition has to contend with the tradition and original calling of Christ. So contending with tradition is crucial to deepening the faith of both individuals and churches.

Struggling with the spiritual, moral, ethical, and doctrinal guidelines of a tradition lets the nourishing power of the tradition sink into our hearts. The natural human desire is to avoid this struggle by choosing only the parts of each tradition that we like. With this selectivity, we never get beyond the beginning of the journey. Instead, we walk around in circles. Avoiding the struggle with tradition also means seeking only peaks and wonders without valleys and deserts. Traditions intentionally guide us to these peaks, yet they also recognize that the route goes by way of the valleys and deserts that help us discover the love and grace of God. Traditions teach us where to look for God, both in the valleys of despair and on the peaks of wonder.

Expect to Be Strengthened

Finally, we have to expect to exercise our faith so that it becomes stronger over the course of our journey. Only as our faith grows stronger can we learn to hold fast to God in every moment.

Life occurs, and in it choices face us every moment. We may use these circumstances to deepen and strengthen our trust in God, or we can trust only ourselves or nothing at all.

I believe God is more interested in *strengthening* us than in *testing* us. Many Christians explain periods of suffering and difficulty as God's testing us. This understanding paints God as a taskmaster whose only concern is whether we pass or fail God's little tests. At its worst, this concept makes God seem cruel and manipulative. For instance, was the Holocaust simply a test of faith for the Jews? No! Were the persecutions of the early Christians simply a test by God to see if they would hold firm to their new religion? No! Were the beatings and bombings that Martin Luther King Jr. and his followers suffered simply a series of "pop quizzes" designed to show how well they had learned? No! Are illnesses, broken relationships, failed ventures, and periods of loneliness and uncertainty heaped upon us by God simply to test the strength of our faith? No!

It is important that we learn in life, but life is not a series of grades and progressions that we have to pass through. Life is both random and purposeful at the same time—the meeting of both free and fixed forces that intersect in each person's life. While God may be in control of life, God does not enslave life.

God has created a wonderful universe that is always in motion and in process. Galaxies swirl; stars and planets dance together; oceans rise and fall; volcanoes erupt; nations form and divide; cultures coalesce and clash; people love and fight; individuals create and destroy. Through it all, God stays with us. God does not have to test us. The material of testing is there all along. Periods of delight and difficulty are present with or without God. Life occurs, and in it choices face us every moment. We may use these circumstances to deepen and strengthen our trust in God, or we can trust only ourselves or nothing at all. The first option strengthens our faith. The other two weaken it. Thus, every moment of life is a moment of potential strengthening.

Robert H. Schuller wrote a book entitled *Tough Times Never Last but Tough People Do!* I disagree with this perspective. While I agree that tough times do not last, I do not necessarily think that tough people last very long either. I think that *faithful* people last. Why? They last because their faith has become tough over the course of the journey. Each moment of struggle, difficulty, turmoil, and uncertainty becomes an opportunity to strengthen faith. The more we forge ahead on the journey of faith, the more faith we need to have.

The key to deepening our faith is to carry realistic expectations of the journey that lies ahead.

God does not cause bad things to occur in life. They happen quite well without God's help. God responds by turning adverse situations into opportunities for us to grow and to strengthen our faith. To grow in faith we have to expect to take advantage of opportunities for strengthening when they occur. Like the author of Hebrews, we must "run with perseverance the race that is set before us, looking to Jesus the pioneer and perfecter of our faith" (Heb. 12:1-2).

The key to deepening our faith is to carry realistic expectations of the journey that lies ahead. One of the underlying themes in the discussion above is that of freedom. We always have the freedom to choose how we will respond to God. Carrying realistic expectations along the journey strengthens our ability to choose God's way over our own.

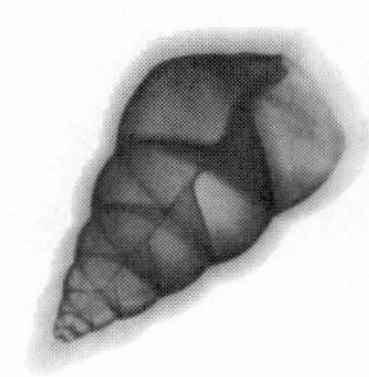

When we travel along the journey of faith, we have to expect an unexpected journey. Life will move in directions we least expect. Moses never expected to be the leader of Jewish salvation. Paul never expected to be the champion of Christian evangelism. Like Moses and Paul, we find that our journeys rarely go where we expect. We have to expect to travel through spiritual deserts and bogs, while being surprised by spiritual peaks and wonders.

The faith journey is rarely an even path. It goes down when we expect it to keep moving upward, and it moves suddenly upward when we feel helplessly stuck on a downward slope.

We also have to expect to share our journey with others. The isolated journey quickly becomes misguided by ignorance, avoidance, and fear. As we share this journey with others, we help ourselves along by engaging in a struggle with our own religious traditions. Traditions show us the way. They help us recognize the path when it is obscure, and they help us appreciate the summit as we gaze outward on God's creation. Finally, by expecting the journey to be filled with opportunities for strengthening, we will forge a deep and lasting faith that can survive any tumult and calamity we may face along the way.

Three
Humble Beginnings

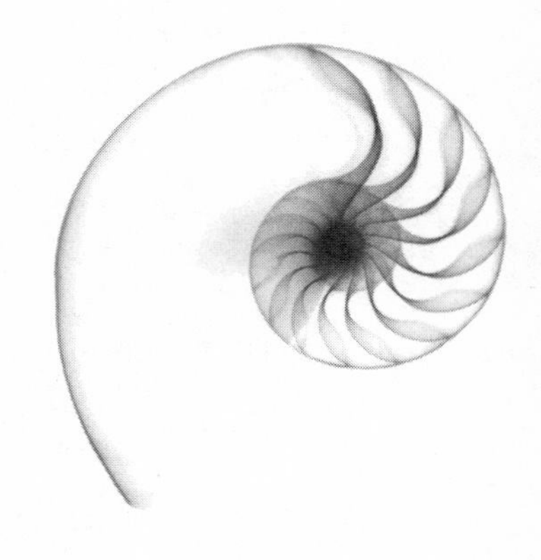

WHILE TAKING a graduate class, I met with a professor to talk about my spiritual struggles. As we talked about my personal prayer life, I told her that I just could not seem to stay focused while praying. I expected her to give me some expert pointers like "Have you tried deep breathing exercises or using visual imagery?" Instead, my professor surprised me with her response. She quietly listened to me chastise myself for not being a better pray-er, and then replied, "Graham, take it easy. Remember, the Apostle Paul had to work on his faith for fourteen years before he was allowed to evangelize. Teresa of Avila [a sixteenth-century mystic] had to use a little prayer book for twenty years because she had such difficulty praying. Give yourself some time. It will come." She was right. I wanted to be at the end of my journey instead of at the beginning. I wanted immediate perfection, and I didn't want to have to go through all the struggles that come with a growing faith.

Generally, we all want to be perfect—or at least better—than we are now. We want to be more accomplished, more proficient, and more in control of our destinies; and we want these things to happen *right now*. This hurriedness is not only part of our human nature; it is an affliction of our technological and instant-gratification age. Too often we try to do things for which we are not ready. In spiritual matters, we try to act out of a faith that we have not yet adequately formed.

In athletics, the good athletes stress the fundamentals that made them good; they continue to work on the basics. My coach in college responded to each loss by having the team members practice the basics until we got it right. We would spend a whole practice doing simple drills that we had done a million times since grade school. He knew that losses often come because we have forgotten to do the basics well.

In forming a strong faith, we also have to keep returning to the basics. If we are going to grow in our faith, we always have to return to our roots—to our beginnings. We have to return to what we really are: beings of this universe who bear a divine spark. We are embodied spirit—divine, yet of the earth. The foundation of spiritual growth is humility. We have to root ourselves in humble beginnings to remain connected to our foundation.

Dirt and Spirit

What are we at our foundation? To find out, it helps to look in the book of Genesis. Genesis 2 beautifully describes humanity: "Then the Lord God formed man from the dust of the ground, and breathed into his nostrils the breath of life; and the man became a living being" (2:7). In the original Hebrew, this first human is *'adam. 'Adam* is formed from the "dust of the ground," or *'adamah.* The source of our humanity is the ground or the earth. In fact, the word *human* literally means "of the ground" (or *humus*). As much as we might try to deny it, we are part of everything around us. At a basic level, there is no difference between me and a lump of clay, a piece of rock, a glass of water, or any other speck of the universe. Thus, becoming humble includes recognizing our humanness—our groundedness in the substance of creation.

What does it mean to you to say that "I am both earth and spirit?"

What does it say to you about your projects, goals, and activities?

Take time to reflect on this.

A distinct human quality allows us to transcend this earthiness. In Genesis, God shapes the first human from the dust of the ground, but God also breathes life into this first human. God's breath, which is God's spirit, gives the first human a spirit. The human is the only creature God creates in this way. The fact that God endows us with spirit distinguishes us from the rest of creation. It is this spirit that makes us distinct. The word *spirit* literally means "breath" or "wind." Thus, when we are in-*spired* by God, we receive God's spirit. When we a-*spire* to God, we seek God's spirit. A fundamental part of being a faithful person is recognizing that we are earthly spirit. C. S. Lewis calls us "amphibians." Just as amphibians breathe water and air, humans inhabit both the timebound earthly realm and the eternal, spiritual realm.[1] We are rooted both in creation and in God, a fact we all too often forget in our hurry to be independent, self-sufficient, and in control.

The Vital Lie

At some level all of us sense our spiritual nature. All but the most stringent atheists recognize our spiritual essence. Unfortunately, we often fail to remember our rootedness in the earthly realm. We easily forget that we are finite, created beings. We act as though we will live forever; yet in reality we exist only for a short period of time. We tend to ignore our earthly nature and create for ourselves a lie that the cultural anthropologist Ernest Becker calls a "vital lie." This vital lie gives us the courage to live in the face of our mortality. Becker says we deny the reality of our mortality and ultimate powerlessness in life.[2] We tell ourselves a vital lie. We pretend to be immortal to avoid the paralyzing fear of death. That fear might prevent our ever taking risks. Feeling immune to the laws of this world gives us the energy and drive to accomplish our tasks. So we set goals for our lives and pursue them as though they mean everything in the world. Becker reminds us that nothing is inherently wrong with the vital lie. But in our present culture this lie has spun out of control. It has led us to worship youth, to spend millions on plastic surgery, to care about ourselves first and others last, and to believe that image is everything while depth is nothing.

How do you feel about the reality that you will die?

Read Ecclesiastes 3. What is your response to these words?

Several years ago, I heard a Dutch psychiatrist talk about how we try so hard to deny our mortality. He said our culture has become obsessed with denying its mortality. He pointed out that while one hundred years ago people also repressed their mortality, the facts of life caused them to face death constantly. People of all ages died of infected scratches, minor illnesses, and accidents at home. Two out of five children would die before age eighteen. The dead were laid out for several days in the home, not a funeral home. Because of death's constant reality, people dealt with it more honestly and openly. Today most deaths seem to occur in old age, often in a hospital or a nursing home. One hundred years ago, people were amazed and thankful to live to an old age. Today it bothers us greatly when people do not. So we hide from our mortality by pursuing strong ambitions that obscure it. We hope that somehow our achievements will defy death.

Ambitions versus Aspirations

Our culture's obsession with youth and immortality has caused us to become a culture of ambition instead of one of aspiration. What does that mean? Adrian van Kaam distinguishes between functional ambitions and spiritual aspirations.[3] Functional ambitions are the goals we set that we hope will give us a sense of control over our lives. These goals and ambitions focus on how well we function in life—on how we execute, manage, and complete tasks. By satisfying these ambitions, we hope people will notice us and reward us with acclaim, higher pay, and more power. Spiritual aspirations, on the other hand, arise out of a desire to discern God's will. When we aspire to something, we seek what God wants. The motivation for achievement arises out of a desire to serve and praise God rather than a desire for praise and reward. When we pursue our aspirations, we seek the guidance of God's spirit.

Ambitions, especially when they consume our lives, rip us from our grounding in creation and our grounding in God by making us believe that we are the center of the universe. Aspirations reconnect us with our ground because they are rooted in the awareness that God is the only eternal in the universe. The balanced spiritual life does not rid life of ambition; it places ambition under the guidance of aspiration. The spiritual person has ambition but is aspiration-led.

The tension between ambition and aspiration reminds me of a disastrous hike I took in New Hampshire while attending summer camp. We were climbing a mountain called Little Haystack. About three-quarters of the way up the mountain is a mass of rock called Shining Rock Cliff—a sharply slanted cliff with streams of water running down its face. Shining Rock Cliff can be seen glistening in the sunlight many miles away. After a relatively easy climb up Little Haystack, we took a break at the base of the cliff. The rock sparkled as spring-fed water gently flowed down its face. It was a fascinating sight.

How can you determine which is your stronger guide: ambitions or aspirations?

Take time to reflect on your motivations. Try to sense the influence of ambition and aspiration in your daily decisions.

Despite our guides' warnings to stay off the cliff, some of the boys were determined to test their rock-climbing skills. Soon three boys were scrambling rapidly up the cliff, ignoring the shouts and orders from the guides. Then disaster hit. One boy, who had managed to climb up about sixty feet, lost his grip and came sliding down the face of the rock. He crashed onto some boulders at the bottom of the cliff and was knocked unconscious. The other two grasped the rock-face in absolute terror. After an hour of waiting, the boys were rescued by guides, who with the help of ropes brought them down safely. We returned to camp in stunned silence as we pondered our mortality. *Could that have been me crashing down on the rocks below? What if that boy had died?* The questions pierced the deepest level of my being.

These ambitious climbers revealed something about human nature that we often overlook or forget: We lose our wisdom when we let ambition consume us. These boys had ambitions of scaling the cliffs. They thought they were immortal. Only when one of them came crashing down did awareness of mortality develop. That awareness terrified us all as we suddenly realized how fragile we really were.

Our culture strongly emphasizes satisfying ambition. The biggest stars of our culture are those who have made it—and made it big. We worship people who have achieved their ambitions, especially if success has made them powerful, rich, or famous. Our biggest celebrities are business people, politicians, musicians, movie stars, and athletes who have defied the odds to achieve what seems like greatness. We generally heap scorn on those who cannot make it—the impoverished, the weak, the uncoordinated, and the misfit.

Openness to God

We all find discomfort in our humanness. It bothers us that none of us possesses anything special except the specialness with which God endows us. My guess is that when Fred Rogers of *Mr. Rogers' Neighborhood* tells each child that she or he is special, Mr. Rogers understands that this specialness derives from the uniqueness of each child—from the fact that each is God's special creation, endowed with God's special gifts. Without God's animating spirit—without that divine spark that lies at our core—we are lumps of inorganic matter. We are a mixture of carbon and water added to a variety of other atoms and molecules. Even as biological creatures, our divine spark distinguishes us from every other creature. We become humble by gaining comfort with our humanness—our mortality, finitude, and ultimate fragility—while recognizing the uniqueness we gain from God's spiritual breath that lies at our core.

How can you become more comfortable with your own humanity and your own mortality?

Take time to talk with God about this.

We grow spiritually in faith by humbling ourselves continually in recognition of our humanness. Many of us believe that being humble means being self-critical, self-effacing, and self-abusing. This is far from the truth. Quaker writer Thomas R. Kelly beautifully describes humility:

> Humility does not rest, in final count, upon bafflement and discouragement and self-disgust at our shabby lives, a brow-beaten, dog-slinking attitude. It rests upon the disclosure of the consummate wonder of God, upon finding that only God counts, that all our self-originated intentions are works of straw. And so in lowly humility we must stick close to the Root and count our own powers as nothing except as they are enslaved in His power.[4]

Humility begins with a rootedness in God—our Root—and our recognition that only God and God's will matter.

To become humble we need to cultivate a sense of fundamental openness to God and God's will. In Christianity, there is a disturbing tendency to substitute ideology, doctrine, dogma, tradition, ritual, mission, and moral codes for actual openness to God. While all of these can deepen our connection with God by teaching us how God wants us to live, they can also close us off to God whenever they become gods and idols in and of themselves.

What are your idols?

Take time to consider honestly what you place in God's place.

Christianity also reminds us that faith in things outside ourselves is not real faith. Real faith forms in the dialogue—the connection—between our hearts with God.

That dialogue opens us to God. The Epistle to the Hebrews reminds us that God's love for us in Jesus Christ has brought the law into our hearts (Heb. 10:16). God's law is not an exterior code but a living, interior, guiding connection with God. Doctrines and codes only have the power to guide us when filtered through our heart's dialogue with God and united with God's call for each of us. We cannot separate Christian theology and mission from our personal sense of God's call. If we separate the two, we may substitute theological teachings and concerns for God's voice, which actually results in our pushing God away.

Do theology, doctrine, or orthodox principles guide your faith?

Or are they your faith?

Take time to reflect on this.

A man once told me that if I was not working with the poor on a full-time basis, I was not really doing God's will. His arrogance closed him to God. Certainly God calls us to care for the poor and the oppressed. However, the man, by making this call a blanket rule for every Christian, substituted the rule for the sensitivity to God's personal call that each of us must have. First we must root our service in our relationship with God. Each person has a unique calling. Only by listening to God can we discover our own calling.

Many people who have rejected Christian faith have tried to create a spirituality that does not include God. Thus, they sever the connection between spirituality and God. Can we be spiritual if we neglect our relationship with God?

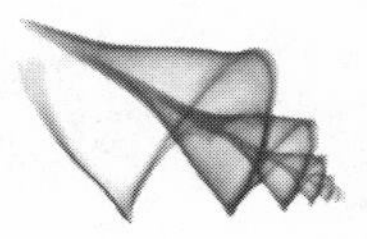

Many current books on spirituality barely mention God. They take a psychomythological approach to spirituality and describe God as some vague truth or essence. Again, can we really be spiritual if we exclude God? Can we form faith without God? My sense is that any spirituality that excludes God's spirit (whether that Spirit is known by a Christian name or not) is by nature nonspiritual. In other words, spirituality needs Spirit. Spirituality requires our openness to God and a desire for God's love. True humility requires a relational openness to God that looks for ways to love God instead of trying to reveal pathways to better living. True humility requires that we actively listen to God, and this listening requires a relationship with God.

True humility requires that we actively listen to God, and this listening requires relationship.

Kelly suggests that humility is actually part of what he calls *holy obedience*.[5] At its root this term literally means holy listening, since obedience at its root means "to listen" or "to hear." When we adopt a sense of holy listening, we humble ourselves by straining to hear what God has to say to us about our life, our path, and our relationship with God. We become open to God. Openness is synonymous with humility.[6] Becoming open to God, God's will, and God's grace is key to setting out on the journey toward God and God's love.

Humble openness begins when we recognize that only God truly matters in life. This stance helps us begin the process of following God humbly along the journey of faith. Our question is this: How we can cultivate a sense of humble openness that leads toward God yet prevents us from blocking God out of our lives?

Obsessed with the Past, Anxious about the Future

A client in therapy with me once told me that he felt "stuck" in a loop with regard to his career. He believed that his father had pushed him into a career. Despite his success, the man felt trapped. He expressed anger about his father's having pushed him in this direction, yet he was not ready to forge a new career at age forty-five. He felt trapped by his past and his future. My client—intellectually bright, temperamentally an achiever, and even-keeled emotionally—was well-suited to his career. He hated the fact that his past fear of displeasing his father had forged his present career. In addition, he feared a future without this career. His present life was shaped by his past and by his fears and anxieties about the future. Thus, he was a product of past memories and future anticipations.[7]

What events from your past dominate and control your life?

Take time to reflect on them, and then offer them to God in prayer. Ask God to help you release them so they don't dominate you.

The past and the future shape us all. Our past experiences shape and form our personalities, habits, and interests. Our anxieties about the future cause us to cling to traits formed by our past, even when destructive. Most of us can say that we "take after" our mother or our father. Beyond that, most of us can also point to specific events that have shaped us and perhaps scarred us. The past helps make us who we are, yet it also can be a prison of our own making when we choose to deny responsibility for our actions by blaming people from the past for our present mistakes.

Ron Rosenbaum satirically calls this tendency to blame our past for our present behavior the ethos of "I can explain that, Maury." He penned the term after writing about an edition of *The Maury Povich Show* in which a professional hit man tried to use his past as justification for his evil actions. After Povich confronted him about his cold-blooded brutality, the man responded, "I can explain that, Maury." He then tried to blame his actions on his childhood. Rosenbaum says, "Talk-show culture has tended to suggest that we can trace all our problems to past abuse of one kind or another, and that once explained, we are absolved. Talk-show culture has been the last refuge of the Enlightenment belief that to understand all is to forgive all."[8] Our past shapes and forms us all to some extent. The question is, how much of our past actually controls us, and how much do we let it control us?

In addition to being dominated by our past, many of us fear taking risks, whether they be small or large. If we risk too much, we might lose a job, a relationship, a way of life, or a cherished way of doing things. I once counseled a young woman who was depressed and had been for several years. What became apparent in counseling was her use of her childhood as an excuse for her depression. While she had had a difficult life and had every reason to feel depressed, being depressed had become a fixed part of her personality and her life. It scared her to think of giving up her depression. Depression gave her an identity, an excuse for every failure in her life. Taking care of her depression became a ten-hour-a-day job as she sought one treatment after another. In a sense, caring for her depression had become her vocation. She glimpsed a future without depression and could not imagine it. She was trapped by her fear of a depression-free life. Her depression was real and needed to be taken care of both medically and psychologically, yet her fear of giving it up magnified the effects. We not only fear future possibilities that may make our lives worse but also those that may make our lives better.

Have there been times in your life when you held on to a destructive way of life, even though you knew it was destructive?

What choices did you have to make to move beyond it?

Take time to reflect on this.

The Freedom to Choose

While both the past and the future exert powerful influences over our lives, we still can exert a certain amount of freedom to choose our own pathways and destinies. God has given us this gift, which separates us from every other thing and creature in God's creation. A rock has no freedom. It is completely controlled by forces of gravity, weather, heat, and cold. Plants are genetically and environmentally controlled. When they receive adequate soil, sun, and water, they grow. Even animals are controlled largely by genetic packaging, instinctual guidance, and environmental conditioning. Only humans have the limited freedom to move beyond their genetics and conditioning. As C. S. Lewis says, human freedom is a gift of God: "Desiring their freedom, [God] therefore refuses to carry them, by their mere affections and habits, to any of the goals… set before them: [God] leaves them to 'do it on their own.'"[9] Thus, while each of us is a constrained and conditioned creature, we also have the freedom to choose other pathways for ourselves.

Inherent in this limited freedom (genetic and social constraints still limit us) lies a choice. God invites us to choose either to live in intimacy with God or to reject God. This may be our most foundational choice. Our lives only become free to the extent that we choose either to follow God or not. If we choose to follow God's way, to some extent we can rise above our genetics and social conditioning. If we do not choose to follow God's way, we end up being controlled and constrained by our biological packaging and the complex conditioning forces of nature, relationships, and society that swirl around us like a hurricane.

Reflect on your life. To what extent have you really been free?

Think of a time when you thought you were making a free choice. What was behind that choice?

What kinds of things were influencing you that you did not even sense?

Take time to pray to God about how to choose God's freedom rather than the illusion of freedom.

There is no such thing as absolute freedom. We choose the main guiding influence in our lives: God or biology and conditioning.

So while our past and future influences and shapes us, we also have a limited freedom to choose between God's pathways and our own constrained and conditioned pathways.

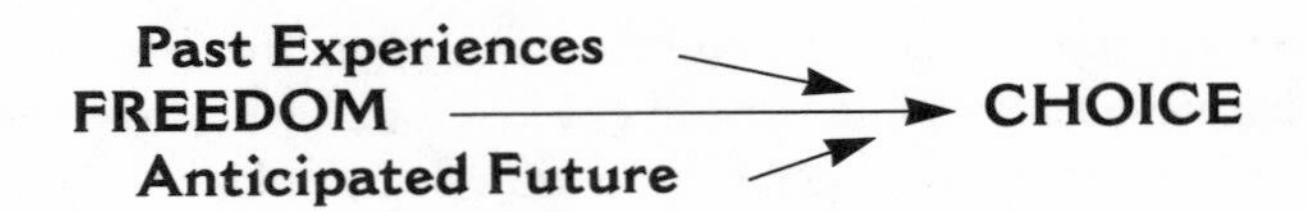

Open or Closed to God's Grace?

We face a choice in every moment of life between being *humbly open to God's grace* or being *closed to God's grace.* Real humility arises from this freedom of choice. We can choose to determine our own pathways in defiance of God and end up serving our ambitions, desires, fears, and need for control. Or we can choose to follow God by recognizing our frailty, contingency, mortality, and our ultimate need for God's guidance. Tales of people who have tried to deny their need for God by attempting to overcome their deep anxieties about powerlessness through force fill the annals of human history, from Alexander the Great, Attila the Hun, and Genghis Khan to Adolf Hitler. These people chose to forge their own grandiose paths, subjecting others to their visions in the process. They may represent the extremes of humanity, but all of us tend to neglect our human need for God to one degree or another. We all feel powerless, and we all want to rise above our basic human constraints to exercise more control.

For example, followers of a man named Charles Paul Brown believe that they can will themselves to be immortal. They believe that by refusing to die, they can create a "cellular awakening" in which they can renew their bodies' cells. We also hear the desire to rise above mortality and humanness expressed by people like Donald Trump, who once said, "I couldn't be happy if I were poor. I'm just too spoiled. Hopefully I won't ever have to deal with it. I think fear drives certain people, and it certainly drives me—the fear of not being able to get what I want."[10] Trump exemplifies the person who would easily relinquish freedom to choose. Fear controls his life, driving him to create a lifestyle that appeases this fear. Fear of the future and the past drives many of us and robs us of choice by controlling us. We all fear loss, and so we try to preserve what we have gained and accomplished. This fear generates overarching ambitions.

Our basic life choice is that of choosing between being controlled by our ambitions or being led by our aspirations. Gerald G. May states the choice in a different way, saying we have a choice between *willingness* and *willfulness*. When we approach life with a sense of willingness, we recognize that we are "part of some ultimate cosmic process," and we freely commit ourselves to this process—we commit ourselves to God's process. When we maintain a willful attitude, we try to set ourselves apart from God's process by trying to control and manipulate it.[11] Our willingness allows God's will to work through us so that more and more, God's will becomes our will. In our willfulness, we place our own aims, goals, and desires—our own will—above God's.

One scripture passage demonstrates the difference between these two life choices. A Canaanite woman asks Jesus to heal her daughter (Matt. 15:21-28). Now, the Canaanites are not Jewish, and the Jews consider them to be unclean and of low character—to be like "dogs." The typical Jew would have sent the woman away. The disciples urge Jesus to do just that. They have ambitions for themselves and for Jesus. They are ushering in the new kingdom that they expect Jesus to bring to Israel. They have no time to waste on this non-Jewish woman, who will never be part of the kingdom: "Send her away, for she keeps shouting after us," the disciples yell to Jesus.

Read Matthew 25:31-46.

What does this passage say about willfulness, willingness, and how you become open or closed to God's grace?

Jesus even seems to agree, "I was sent only to the lost sheep of the house of Israel. It is not fair to take the children's food and throw it to the dogs." In effect, he says, "Woman, you aren't part of my plans. I'm here to save the Jews, not you lowly Canaanites." The woman's reply surprises them: "Yes, Lord, yet even the dogs eat the crumbs that fall from their masters' table." That statement touches Jesus' heart. In an example of true willingness, Jesus expresses God's love for the woman by exclaiming, "Woman, great is your faith! Let it be done for you as you wish." Her daughter receives healing.

While humanity has a serious problem with willfulness, many people also cut themselves off from God's grace through *willlessness,* the relinquishment of freedom to choose by allowing another person, group, or movement to dominate their lives.[12] These persons lack a sense of self-worth and let another's ambitions guide them, which may lead to abuse or manipulation.

To what extent are you willful in your life?

To what extent are you willing?

Take time to reflect on how much your life is centered on your own will and how much it is centered on God's will.

Will-less people tend to match up with willful people. They enter into a relationship in which one person who has the illusion of freedom grows stronger by crushing the freedom of another. It is difficult to overcome will-lessness because will-less people do not know how to become more willing. Their experience is limited to their own will-lessness or another's willfulness. God's will never dominates. God is not willful, so choosing to let God's will flow through us is not easy if we have been will-less. Seeking God's will means seeking a gentle will. Surrounded by so many others who will exert their will on our behalf makes the discernment of God's will all the harder. Will-less persons need to forge a sense of confidence in their ability to hear and follow God, a difficult task when they have little or no confidence.

In what areas do you allow others to dominate you?

Do you struggle with will-lessness?

How might you become more willing?

Take time to pray to God to guide you.

Willfulness causes us to close ourselves off to God's grace by convincing us to follow our own ambitions. Will-lessness closes us off to God's grace by convincing us to give in to the will of others—to permit a person, group, or movement to dominate us. When we are willing, however, we open ourselves to God's grace because we follow our aspirations and the Holy Spirit's inspirations, which guide and reform our ambitions.

OPEN TO GOD'S GRACE

willingness

guided by aspirations

Past Experiences →
FREEDOM → **CHOICE**
Anticipated Future →

guided or dominated by ambitions

willfulness / will-lessness

CLOSED TO GOD'S GRACE

Choose Freedom

We constantly choose between willingly opening ourselves up to God's grace and willfully closing ourselves off to God's grace. This choice comes with every moment of life. The mystics and spiritual leaders throughout Christianity's history have always understood this idea of constant choice. Devoting and uniting our will to God is a continual life choice. It is the core of our humility. Only in true humility can we place our will before the Creator at every moment, which is exactly what Jesus does with the Canaanite woman. He keeps his heart continually open to God's will and unites his will with God's. This openness to God's will brings the power of healing. God's grace flows through Jesus because he is humbly open to doing God's will. The disciples, on the other hand, stubbornly cling to their own will, wanting glory and power, not grace.

When we choose to close ourselves off to God's grace, we also limit our sense of freedom. Closing ourselves to God and following our own ambitions create a sense of security, independence, and self-reliance. Ironically in choosing to forge our own course by shutting God out of our lives, our past and our future control us even more. We find ourselves locked into particular patterns of behavior and cycles of response that eventually control us. The disciples, like we, allowed their desire for power, glory, notoriety, and security to control them. In his teaching, Jesus always had to remind them that it is God who matters. He continually had to show them (and us) that when we lock God out of our daily life, we rob ourselves of freedom and choice.

Reflect on your life and on a time when you were closed to God. What guided your life—past experiences, future anxieties and desires?

How did opening yourself to God change things?

In present-day Bethlehem, the priests and monks who take care of the Church of the Nativity reflected this internal conflict. This reputed site of Jesus' birth is maintained jointly by the Armenian, Orthodox, Greek Orthodox, and Roman Catholic Churches. The priests and monks of each tradition maintain a particular portion of the church. In the 1980s a fight broke out when an Orthodox monk climbed a ladder and cleaned a beam in the Armenian part of the church. Immediately priests and monks from both sides pulled out chains and clubs hidden in their robes and attacked one another as they protected their "turf." Why did this happen? They had allowed past prejudices and future fears to control them. In their anger over past conflicts and fear of losing control over the church, they shut out God's call to live together in Christian love. Both sides had given up their freedom to choose God's will.

We tend to ignore God's call whenever we rigidly and idolatrously adopt certain ideological, philosophical, theological, and moral perspectives. While these perspectives help us learn how to live in more meaningful ways, we may substitute them for God.

The danger always exists that we will make them rigid idols by believing that our views and beliefs are those of God. That idolatry encourages criticism of Christians for being hypocrites. Christians may follow the rituals and practices of Christianity, but an obsession with particular practices actually can close them to God's spirit. Keeping open hearts takes effort. It is much easier to substitute a belief, a practice, or a code of living for God. Theology and morality should lead us to God, rather than become gods themselves.

Greater freedom and choice often bring a sense of struggle and suffering.

When we choose to open ourselves willingly to God's grace and will, we also open ourselves to greater freedom and choice. Although this openness may seem like a wonderful thing, most of us do not experience it that way. Greater freedom and choice often bring a sense of struggle and suffering. Our radical openness to God's grace moves us in directions that are unknown and therefore uncomfortable. Our openness to God's grace can bring an overwhelming range of possibilities. We want predictability, but following God is never predictable. Openness to God often immerses us in uncertainty and ambiguity. On the other hand, being closed to God feels more comfortable because it gives us the illusion of certainty, the illusion that we are in control.

What examples can you think of that illustrate how theological concerns and moral codes have closed you to God and God's voice?

Jesus offers the classic example of the struggle that comes with opening ourselves to God when he prays in the Garden of Gethsemane before his arrest and crucifixion. In the garden, Jesus grapples with the deep pain and turmoil that often accompanies radical openness to God. Mark's Gospel tells us that Jesus is "distressed and agitated," saying to Peter, James, and John, "I am deeply grieved, even to death" (Mark 14:34). Luke's Gospel reports that Jesus' "sweat became like great drops of blood falling down on the ground" (Luke 22:44). Jesus prays that God will remove "this cup"—this course leading to his death—from him. Yet in the end Jesus chooses to follow God's will, not his own (Luke 22:42). To be humbly open to God means becoming immersed in a painful struggle with uncertainty—with the fact that we only see through the glass darkly (1 Cor. 13:12). We prefer our paths of safety and predictability. Choosing to follow God's path generally leads to the discomfort of change and transformation.

Truth

Ultimately, choosing to be humbly open to God's grace deepens our lives, even in the midst of suffering, by moving us away from the surface of life and into the depths of truth about life's meaning and God's desires. Our openness to God's grace also opens us to the truth revealed through freedom and choice.

The road to this truth generates discomfort because we discover truths about ourselves and the nature of life that we do not want to know. Anthony de Mello says, "The Truth that sets us free is almost always the Truth we would rather not hear."[13] This kind of truth may deepen our lives, but it also makes our lives more painful until we become used to the revealed truth. Paul Tillich suggests that suffering is the only door that leads to the depth of truth: "It is comfortable to live on the surface so long as it remains unshaken. It is painful to break away from it and to descend into unknown ground."[14] When we seek truth, we descend into unknown ground and choose to remain there. The descent does not bring permanent pain. Over time, the pain melts away into joy as we form a deeper life with God.

Do you want to become more open to God in your life?

Take time to pray with God about this, and listen for God's response.

What does humbly opening ourselves to truth look like on a practical level? One man who had never really been religious told me that he joined a Bible study after several of his clients died in a devastating plane crash near Pittsburgh. The crash opened him to God in a radical and humbling way, changing his life and leading him to take his life and relationships more seriously.

After years of unsuccessful attempts to have a child with the help of fertility drugs and in-vitro fertilization, a friend of mine finally gave it all up to God. She decided to accept whatever God had in store for her life. If that meant not having children, then she would serve God in another way. An amazing thing happened: Within two months of opening her life to God, she became pregnant. Now she has two children. She was blessed to have a healing experience, but she also would have accepted another outcome. She displayed an openness to God. I realize that other women have had similar hopes that did not come to fulfillment in this way. Yet this story points out that we are called to open ourselves to God in all the different conditions of life.

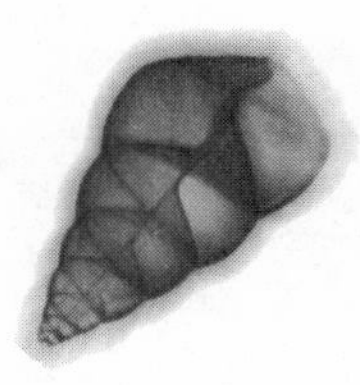

Another friend decided to use rush-hour traffic as an opportunity to pray daily with God. As a result, he began to recognize God's presence even in the mundane moments of life.

Listening to God in the Present

These people let go of their past and their future to focus on listening to God in the present. Only when we open ourselves to God in the present are we truly open to the Spirit's guidance. As Jean-Pierre de Caussade, an eighteenth-century priest, wrote, "It is necessary to be disengaged from all we feel and do in order to walk with God in the duty of the present moment. All other avenues are closed. We must confine ourselves to the present moment without taking thought for the one before or the one to come."[15] The road to discovering God's will lies in detachment from the anxieties of our past and from our fears about the future so that we can listen to God in the *now*. Only when we live with God in the present moment do we begin to connect with the eternal realm. As C. S. Lewis says, "[God] therefore, I believe, wants them to attend chiefly to two things, to eternity itself and to that point at which time touches eternity. For the Present is the point at which time touches eternity."[16] Whenever we let go of our past and our future, even for a moment, to listen to God in the present, we are living in eternity. Humility is the doorway that leads to eternity, for in that moment we become open to God.

What truths about yourself have you avoided acknowledging in the past?

At what times have you tried to follow God's will and had them lead to confusion and struggle?

Take time to reflect on these situations.

I have developed a practice of listening to God in the present, and it has become a powerful spiritual tool in my life. I use it when I deeply want to seek God's will but am overwhelmed by my fears, ambitions, and desires. I take time for quiet and center upon God. Then I ask God what God would have me do. I ignore the first voice I hear because it is usually my fears and emotions speaking. Then I ignore the second voice because it is usually my mind trying to guess what God wants. I continue the process by trying to let go of all my ambitious and fearful thoughts and emotions. Finally, I begin to hear a quiet and calm voice at my center—not an audible voice, but one that gives direction. I find that by listening to this voice, I come closest to listening to God's voice. I am not so arrogant as to believe that this voice is God's, but I am convinced that this small voice is connected to the spiritual realm. Also before acting on what I sense, I try to let it set for a while. If it is of God, it grows in strength. If not, it fades.

On a practical level, becoming humbly open to God means openly inviting God to speak to us and trusting that God will guide us along our unpredictable faith journey. Humble openness can lead both to mundane and miraculous ways of living with God. Then the model of humble openness looks like this:

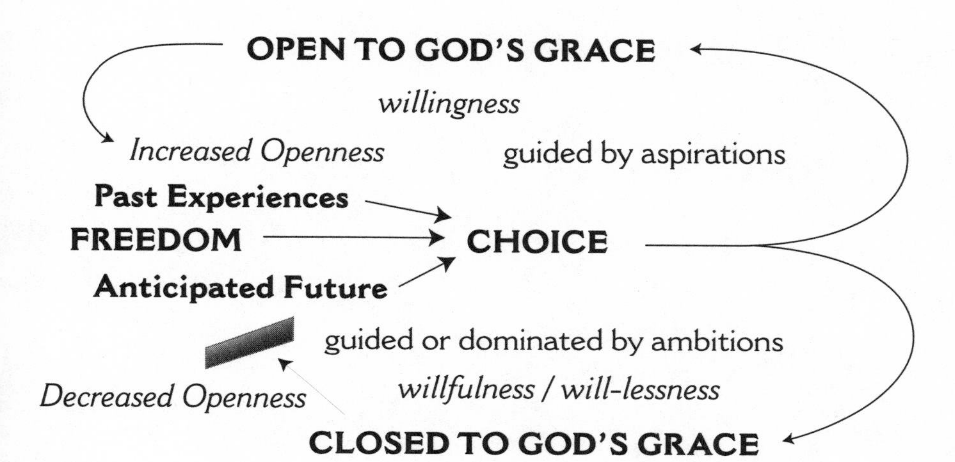

So while our biological, psychological, and social past controls our lives to some extent as well as our fears and expectations of the future, we always have a certain amount of freedom. We face this choice in each moment of life. Do we open or close ourselves to God's grace?

By opening ourselves to God's grace, we increase our level of freedom—sometimes with overwhelming effect. An increased sense of freedom can bring with it a sense of suffering and confusion because it leads us into unknown territory. Eventually, the unknown path gives way to joy as we sense God more intimately in our lives. Closing ourselves off to God's grace may heighten our feelings of security, yet it is a false security based on the fragility, weakness, and mortality of humans.

Do you open or close yourself to God's grace?

In what ways do you do that?

Becoming humble means recognizing that we are God's creation and that God created us to live in intimate relationship with God. We may turn away from God in order to forge our own independent pathways. Humility calls us to break free of the human tendency to isolate ourselves from God and to open our hearts to God's grace and love. Only in this way can we set ourselves on the journey of faith. Humility orients us and keeps us focused on what matters and what does not. It also leaves us open to God's grace as it leads us along the journey of faith.

Four

Speaking and Listening

WHEN I WAS eight years old, I remember walking out to my favorite tree and praying. I remember this moment vividly, as though it happened only a few years ago. It was my favorite tree because I could shinny up its trunk easily. I would wrap my arms and legs around the tree and pull myself up to the top. Then I would cling to the top and look around feeling strong.

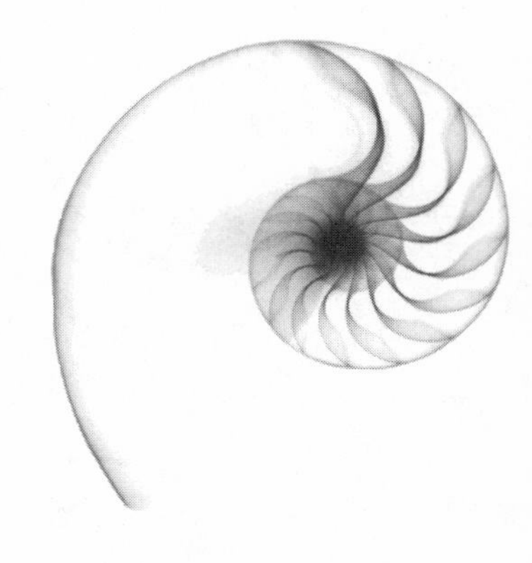

On that particular day, I climbed to the top and surveyed my kingdom. I thought about my great love for the trees, the fields, and all the animals. Soon I slid down the tree and looked back up at the spindly branches near the top. Then I prayed to God: "God, let me always be kind to animals. Help me always love animals and treat them well. And let them always know that I love them."

Why do I remember this prayer so clearly? Probably because it was my first truly deep prayer, the first time that I had prayed from my heart. This prayer also served as the first time I had prayed and felt changed because of it. My prayer had a depth that I had never experienced before, as if I had moved from one degree of life to another. In that moment, I became deeply aware of God's presence, and I knew that God would help me change my life so that I could love creation more fully.

When have you experienced a closeness to God?

What was going on in your life?

How did this experience differ from others?

Take time to reflect on this.

I had moved from one way of relating with God to a deeper one. Before, my relationship with God had always been more dutiful and shallow. I prayed before bedtime; I prayed at the dinner table; or I prayed in church. God seemed distant, and prayer stemmed from duty. I had never realized that I could form a personal relationship with God. Relating to God was the business of priests and pastors. Besides, I was just a kid. But in this moment beside the tree, I entered into a dialogue with God; and I knew that God had heard me.

Prayer as Dialogue

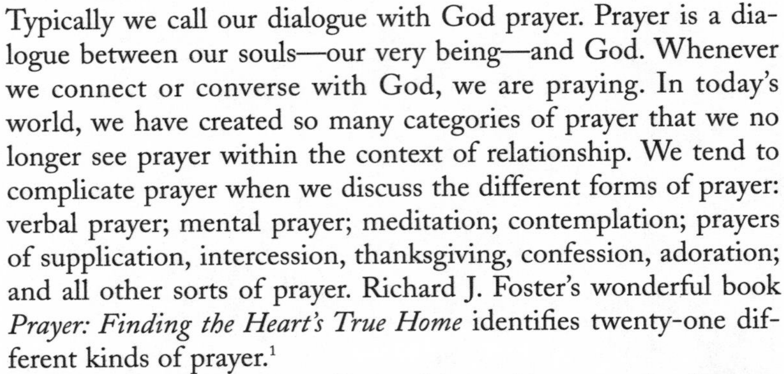

Typically we call our dialogue with God prayer. Prayer is a dialogue between our souls—our very being—and God. Whenever we connect or converse with God, we are praying. In today's world, we have created so many categories of prayer that we no longer see prayer within the context of relationship. We tend to complicate prayer when we discuss the different forms of prayer: verbal prayer; mental prayer; meditation; contemplation; prayers of supplication, intercession, thanksgiving, confession, adoration; and all other sorts of prayer. Richard J. Foster's wonderful book *Prayer: Finding the Heart's True Home* identifies twenty-one different kinds of prayer.[1]

Yet despite the many different forms of prayer, at its foundation prayer is simply our ongoing dialogue with God, the "stuff" of our relationship with God. The different forms of prayer strongly resemble the various ways we relate with one another. Sometimes we talk at length about our concerns while others listen. Sometimes we listen while others tell us about their hopes and dreams for life. Sometimes we sit with others in silence, sharing an unspoken dialogue that makes words unnecessary. At other times our dialogue with others is brief and more to the point.

Whatever form we use, prayer is the ongoing conversation between ourselves and God. The German spiritual theologian Hans Urs von Balthasar says, "Prayer *is* a conversation between God and the soul, and secondly, a particular language *is* spoken: God's language. Prayer *is* dialogue, not [humanity's] monologue before God."[2] To go a step further, we do not initiate the dialogue of prayer—God does. We respond to God's beckoning deep in our hearts by entering an ever-deepening dialogue with God. My dialogue with God began as an eight-year-old. At that moment beside the tree, I responded to something from God deep within my heart that urged me to pray. At that moment, God invited me to share my love for God's creation.

Reflect on your prayers.

Do you find yourself engaging in a dialogue with God?

How can you make your prayer more of a relationship?

Take time to ask God about this in prayer.

As prayer becomes more important to us, we progressively deepen our relationship with God and discover more about who God is and who we are. When we pray, we open ourselves to God and discover how much God loves us, how present God is in our lives, and how much God calls to us.

When we do not pray, we can easily lose our way as we travel the journey of faith, which is a journey of falling more deeply in love with God. Prayer plunges us into the depths of God's love. The more we pray, the more we learn to cherish God. We become more sensitive to God's deep love and care for us. At the same time, prayer helps us see ourselves through God's eyes. We see our own faults and flaws more clearly. This perspective encourages us to live more and more by God's grace.

Prayer is the dialogue of humility, the continuous process of opening ourselves to God and God's grace. As we pray more deeply and more often, our love for God expands as our relationship with God grows. If faith is primarily a journey of learning to love God, then prayer is the language of love. As our love for God deepens, we desire more time in prayer; prolonged periods without prayer leave us feeling empty. Thus, prayer deepens our love and longing for God, and our love and longing for God deepen our prayer.

How Can We Love What We Do Not Know?

This talk about falling in love with God raises a fundamental problem. A group of teenagers were talking about how to hold onto their faith after graduating from high school. One of the girls in the group asked a question that drives right to the heart of the problem we all have with prayer: "How can we love God if we never hear God? How do we love a God we don't know?" Her question was beautiful in its simplicity and honesty: How do we love God if we do not know God?

This question highlights the fact that love emerges only in relationship. Can we love anyone or anything we do not know? Anthony de Mello tells a story that illustrates the difficulty of caring about anyone we do not know. A friend came to the famous essayist Charles Lamb and said, "I want to introduce you to Mr. So-and-So." "No, thank you," Lamb replied. "I don't like the man." "But you don't even know him!" "I know. That is why I don't like him," said Lamb.[3]

Lamb hit the nail on the head. It is hard to like someone we do not know. It is even harder to *love* those we do not know. The same is true regarding our relationship with God. We cannot love God if we do not know God.

The real struggle with prayer has to do with how we come to know God. As long as we demand that God use a human voice, we will always be frustrated because God is not limited to human

In what ways do you struggle with prayer?

Does part of your struggle have to do with a sense that you never hear God in your prayers?

Read Matthew 26:36-46.

Does Jesus see or hear God?

Reflect on what the story may say about how you do hear God.

voices. God speaks through sunsets, stars, television shows, music, a cross, people, books, pets, children, and many other avenues. We have trouble hearing God in prayer because we are so limited in the ways we listen. We cannot love God unless we know God, and we cannot know God unless we hear God. Hearing God requires that we become more sensitive to God, and to become more sensitive we have to desire a deep, loving relationship with God that we express in our daily lives. We have to want to share our daily lives with God. We have to want to hear God in a leaf, a song on the radio, and the smile of a friend; and we have to want to be open to God and share our lives with God.

The Inner Conflict

Once again we return to the issue of relationship, which drives to the heart of our difficulty in hearing or knowing God. We do not know God because we resist forming a relationship with God. Through lack of relationship, we lose our sensitivity to God's presence. Love comes only in relationship, yet we tend to push God away even while desiring God's greater involvement in our lives. We find ourselves engaged in an inner conflict. We want God to be involved—but not too involved. We want God to be a presence—but not too present. We want God to act in our lives during periods of turmoil and struggle and to leave us alone when things are going well. We desire intimacy with God, but we want our space.

Reflect on your relationship with God.

Do you easily and naturally turn to God?

Do you keep God on the fringes of your life?

Paul Tillich says that this conflict arises from the pull both of our human sinfulness and God's grace. We tend to think of sin as a failure to follow certain prohibitions and commands.[4] To many Christians, sin is smoking, drinking, swearing, fighting, and other moral lapses. This view of sin ignores the fundamental nature of sin, which according to Tillich, is not really bad behavior. Sin is actually the estrangement or separation that arises between us and God whenever we make ourselves the center of the universe.[5] This egoism leads to the behaviors that we traditionally label as sinful. By making ourselves the center of life, we turn from God and let selfish ambition, addiction, and attachment take control of our lives.

The fact that we recognize our tendency to push God away demonstrates God's refusal to be pushed away. God pursues us despite our pushing away. God wants to be part of our lives and evokes in our hearts a deep longing for God. While we push away from God, God reminds us of our reason for being: to share our lives with God. The fact that we seek God in prayer, especially during times of trouble and turmoil, suggests that at our core we know we need God. The result is a fragmented relationship with God: We seek God and ignore God, love God and are indifferent to God, accept God's will and reject it.

Over time our acceptance of God's love for us and our offering of love to God in return helps heal our fragmented relationship with God. Prayer becomes a major part of the healing process. It heals the fractures that separate God and us. Through prayer, we discover God's activity in our lives as we become increasingly more sensitive to God and God's presence. We learn to recognize God in actions, symbols, rituals, thoughts, relationships, feelings, events, and experiences. As we expand our dialogue with God, we deepen our love for God.

Do you find yourself in the midst of a conflicted relationship with God in which you push God away as you invite God's closeness?

Take time to reflect on your relationship with God.

Cycles of Prayer

All relationships move in cycles, marked by varying kinds of intimacy. For instance, people who barely know one another relate in a casual way. Little dialogue takes place between them other than introductions and small talk. Closer relationships have more intimate ways of relating. Each way of relating has its own patterns and practices—its own cycle of activities.

As we get to know someone, we become more interested in his or her response to us. As our feelings become stronger, we may develop a fascination or infatuation with the person. We want to spend more time listening as we learn more and discover how his or her life converges with ours. When we share a strong love, we do not have to share words. Just being together is often enough. Facial gestures, body postures, and the shared space between people keeps the dialogue alive with little need for verbal conversation.

These various ways of relating also exist in our relationship with God. They become the different *cycles of praying* that we move through as we deepen our relationship.

Often we get caught up in the ways of "doing" prayer rather than remembering the focus on relationship. This can cause people to turn prayer into a rigid activity full of rules rather than a natural connection between them and God. Two women I know found the suggestion of praying while sitting cross-legged with palms facing upward disturbing. To them, this posture seemed an un-Christian way of praying. Actually, no prescribed Christian way of praying exists. The prophets of old prayed sitting down with their head between their legs. The desert fathers and mothers, members of Christian sects that lived in the deserts of Egypt during the fourth and fifth centuries, prayed while sitting cross-legged. The monastics of the Middle Ages often prayed while lying face down with outstretched arms in imitation of Jesus on the cross. The followers of the Hesychastic tradition of the Eastern Orthodox Church uttered a constant prayer, "Lord Jesus Christ, have mercy on me," while going about their daily routine. They were following the Apostle Paul's admonition to "pray constantly" (1 Thess. 5:17). As a child, I learned to pray on my knees with my hands clasped together in front of me.

Often we get caught up in the ways of "doing" prayer rather than remembering the focus on relationship.

So while no particular way of praying to God is the "right" way, different cycles of praying reflect the kinds of encounters we have with God. As our relationship with God changes and as our emphasis changes, our ways of praying change. Each cycle incorporates the previous ways of praying, while moving us to other cycles. The different cycles give us a sense of what matters in our relationship with God and also help us appraise the kind of relationship our churches, communities, or groups have with God. The four cycles—thinking, speaking, listening, and loving—together form the larger cycle of prayer.

Thinking Cycle

In this first cycle of relating with God, we think about God and acknowledge God as creator and sustainer of the universe, but our relationship remains distant. We have little direct contact with God. This does not mean that we do not have faith or that we lack a sense of spiritual depth. While we may not have moved to a more intimate way of relating with God, we still *think* about the need for God. The distance in relationship comes because we have not emphasized intimacy with God. We emphasize observing God and God's work from a detached perspective.

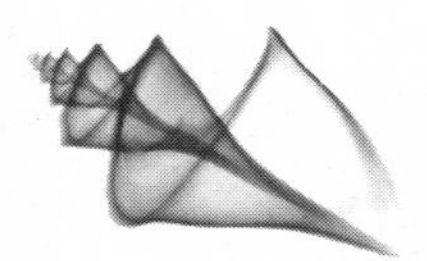

As long as we remain in the *thinking cycle,* we regard God as somewhat distant, aloof, and apart from our world—a common conception of God for many people. We investigate our lives and consider ourselves to be on our own to some extent. We may recognize God's existence without perceiving God's involvement in daily, mundane events of life.

This concept of God, which views God as incapable of suffering and feeling, considers God part of the divine realm, not the earthly realm. It emerged out of the philosophies of the ancient Greek philosophers Plato and Aristotle, and it slowly began to influence Christianity in the second and third centuries C.E.[6] From this perspective, we believe that we only connect with God when we die.

Thinking

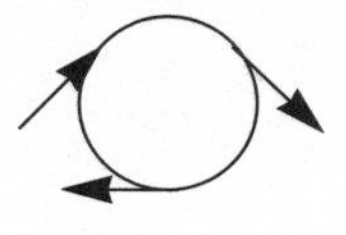

In the thinking cycle of prayer, thinking about God theologically and participating in formal worship is the extent of our prayer. We have little direct contact with God. While we may think quite a bit about God, wonder about God's nature, and consider all sorts of basic theological questions, we rarely pray directly to God. When prayer occurs, it takes place in worship or in some other formal setting.

Many of us churchgoers fit this description. While we may regularly attend worship, serve on committees and boards, give money, and try to live by the Golden Rule of treating others as we would be treated, we still see God as being unconnected to our lives. God is a distant observer who waits for us to die so that God can either embrace us or judge us or both.

Do you operate primarily out of a thinking mode?

How heavily do you rely on this form of prayer?

Reflect on how this approach connects with your beliefs about God.

Many clergy seem to go no further than this cycle of relating with God. They relate to God through their intellect, reading scripture, sermons, and books on theology. They think about God quite a bit. Yet they rarely pray except to pray formally during the worship service. These clergy feel too much distance between them and God. They feel dry and useless when they pray, so they allow their thinking, reasoning, and ministry activities to become their prayer.

Being critical of people who relate to God solely through this cycle ignores the fact that thinking about God is still a legitimate way of praying. It is a more distant, cautious, and formal way of relating, yet it is still relating. In fact, resting in this cycle at times can be important for all of us. It gives us a sense of space from God and a sense of perspective. At times, we need to explore our own individuality apart from God. This space helps us nurture the unique gifts God has given us.

One danger of today's emphasis on prayer and spirituality is a tendency to believe that rational and theological thinking is bad, while spiritually feeling God's presence is good. Yet both are

How do you envision God?

Does God seem distant and aloof?

Take time to reflect on your perception.

necessary. At times it is appropriate to sit back and rationally reflect on the words of scripture, on theological issues, and on the meaning of our lives. At other times, it is better to plunge into our relationship with God by allowing ourselves to seek after and experience God's presence. A problem arises when we remain fixed in the thinking cycle of prayer without nurturing other forms of relating with God.

An example of being fixated in the thinking cycle comes in Matthew's Gospel as Jesus criticizes those who make a show of their praying:

> "And whenever you pray, do not be like the hypocrites; for they love to stand and pray in the synagogues and at the street corners, so that they may be seen by others. Truly I tell you, they have received their reward. But whenever you pray, go into your room and shut the door and pray to your Father who is in secret; and your Father who sees in secret will reward you" (Matt. 6:5-6).

Take a look at your own prayer life.

When has thinking about God been helpful for you?

Why is it important to think theologically and reflectively?

This scripture is probably one of the more misunderstood passages of the Bible. Many people interpret it as Jesus' condemnation of public prayer, but it is not. Jesus speaks against prayer that is shallow and only for show. Public prayer is vitally important and can lead us into deeper ways of relating with God. But when prayer stays formal and distant, our relationship with God also stays formal and distant rather than becoming mutual and intimate. To grow deeper in our relationship with God, we need to explore the other cycles of prayer.

Speaking Cycle

As Jesus' criticism of the hypocrites shows, we are always called to move to other ways of prayer, forging a deeper relationship with God. We are invited to speak with God about our lives. When we move through a *speaking cycle* of prayer, we not only think about God, but we also ask God to become a force in our lives. We become aware that God is not distant and aloof, but instead God actively participates in our daily living. Because we become aware that God listens to us and cares deeply about us, we speak to God about our struggles, hopes, problems, joys, and concerns. In effect, when we engage in the speaking cycle, we ask God to become an active, more intimate part of our lives.

This cycle of prayer is in harmony with Jesus' teaching on prayer. He says,

> "Ask, and it will be given you; search, and you will find; knock, and the door will be opened for you. For everyone who asks receives, and everyone who searches finds, and for everyone who knocks, the door will be opened. Is there anyone among you who, if your child asks for bread, will give a stone? Or if the child asks for a fish, will give a snake? If you then, who are evil, know how to give good gifts to your children, how much more will your Father in heaven give good things to those who ask him!" (Matt. 7:7-11).

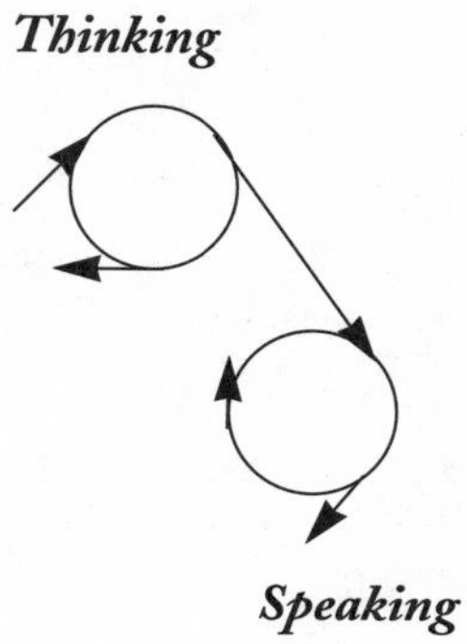

Thinking

Speaking

Apparently, God wants us to ask, search, and knock. God wants us to seek divine help, so that God can act in our lives.

While I do not believe that this kind of praying is intended as a vehicle to convince God to help us win the lottery or to help our favorite football team score a touchdown, I am convinced that God wants us to pray for things that are important to us. By calling on God to intervene in our lives, we forge a stronger connection with God.

Agnes Sanford comments that God's activity in our lives is directly related to how willing we are to accept God's activity in our lives. She says, "And just as a whole world full of electricity will not light a house unless the house itself is prepared to receive that electricity, so the infinite and eternal life of God cannot help us unless we are prepared to receive that life within ourselves. *Only the amount of God that we can get in us will work for us.*"[7] Speaking more to God about our daily concerns allows God to become a greater force in our lives. We move beyond just thinking about God and actively call on God to have a greater impact on our lives.

How comfortable do you feel with asking God for something?

If uncomfortable, try asking God in prayer to help you become more comfortable.

Then try making specific requests of God for your life, someone else's life, or in the world.

An old saying states that there are no atheists in foxholes. Most people want God to influence their lives whenever their lives (or their lifestyles) are threatened. We ask God to heal an illness; help us find a job; mend a broken relationship; show us a new path; get us out of a crisis; and help the hungry, the hurting, and the oppressed. As Jesus makes clear, God expects us to ask and to knock. Again, the problem with this cycle of praying is that we can get stuck here and resist moving any deeper in our relationship with God.

When we remain fixed in the speaking cycle of praying, there is a danger that we will see God as a personal genie, especially if we have an overly pietistic faith. We may relate to God in a self-centered way and expect God to change to meet our wishes and desires. This kind of approach to God actually uses a sophisticated method of resisting God. We are willing to remain faithful to God as long as God fulfills our wishes, but we refuse to change one bit to meet God's call for us. Thus, we resist the transformation of our hearts and become frustrated by God's refusal to answer our prayers in the ways we desire.

Read Luke 11:5-13. What does this passage say to you about speaking to God?

When we get fixed or stuck in a speaking way of praying, we can become intolerant of God's failure to do our will. We may try to get God's attention by praying louder, using more flowery and religious language, or simply holding back our prayers as a way of punishing God. We may not recognize the fact that since we are not approaching God from a humbly open perspective, we inhibit our ability to sense God's response. While the speaking cycle of praying is a good and important cycle, it becomes problematic when we are unwilling to immerse ourselves in other cycles. Our speaking needs the balance of listening.

Listening Cycle

The book of First Kings tells how the great prophet Elijah chastises King Ahab for allowing the Israelites to worship the god Baal (1 Kings 18:30–19:18). To show Ahab how misguided this worship is, Elijah, the lone prophet of God, asks Ahab to gather all 450 of Baal's prophets on the top of Mount Carmel. Elijah then challenges them to a duel: Baal's prophets are to call on Baal to light their sacrificial fire. Elijah will call on God. So the prophets build their fire. Then comes the time to produce. Baal's prophets pray and chant, but nothing happens. Elijah laughs at them and then pours buckets of water on his pile of wood, drenching it. How can anyone light a fire so wet? But when Elijah calls upon God to light his fire, it bursts into flame. Afterward, Elijah mocks the other prophets for their failure. Ahab, in a fit of embarrassment and rage, puts all of Baal's prophets to death.

Elijah's mockery of her religion makes Ahab's wife, Jezebel (a worshiper of Baal), furious. Her threats to kill Elijah leave him no choice but to flee. He despairs of having taken this great stand for God, for now it seems that he will die because of it.

God's prophets often found that following God's call led them into turmoil and danger. We may have similar experiences. We try to follow Christ's call; but when we do, our lives become more difficult. At these times we have to be willing to listen even more deeply to God.

Elijah does just that. He listens more deeply. To escape Jezebel, he flees south to Judah and from there into the wilderness for forty days and nights. Eventually he comes to Mount Horeb where he quiets his heart and listens for God:

> Now there was a great wind, so strong that it was splitting mountains and breaking rocks in pieces before the Lord, but the Lord was not in the wind; and after the wind an earthquake, but the Lord was not in the earthquake; and after the earthquake a fire, but the Lord was not in the fire; and after the fire a sound of sheer silence. When Elijah heard it, he wrapped his face in his mantle and went out and stood at the entrance of the cave (1 Kings 19:11-13).

Apparently Elijah hears something in the silence that causes him to stand up and walk out to the cave entrance—something that he did not hear in the wind, earthquake, or fire. What does he hear? He hears God in the silence. He hears God in the depths of his heart, and this hearing bolsters his ability to follow God with confidence. We might have expected to hear God in the great cataclysmic events of the earth, wind, or fire; yet there is something profound in the fact that Elijah hears God only in the silence. How often do we hear God in the quiet moments of life?

Elijah was not only adept at speaking to God, but he also was willing to *listen* deeply for God. In that mountain cave Elijah moved from the *speaking* to the *listening* cycle of prayer. When we pray in this cycle, it is not enough just to speak to God and expect God to act. We also remain open to God's continual call to us. When we listen, we yearn for God to be an intimate part of our lives and willingly open our lives to God. We realize that prayer does not mean getting God to change life to meet our needs but that we need to change our lives to follow God's call.

At what times in your life have you heard God?

Reflect on how God spoke to you.

How did you recognize God's voice?

Listening for God requires a special and, for most of us, a different kind of listening. Typically when we listen, we try to gain as much information as we can before deciding on a course of action. This is the consumer approach to living. Before we buy a car we compare makes and models to determine what we want, then shop around for the right price. There is nothing wrong with this approach. Certain aspects of life demand that we gain enough information to make wise decisions.

Today's Western culture is an information culture. Information constantly floods our lives. Television, radio, magazines, and newspapers keep us posted on what has taken place in politics, society, sports, and our local communities. The Internet gives us information about everything we could possibly need and even about things we do not need. Unfortunately, all this information can hinder our spiritual development. It can make listening to God more difficult. Listening to God does not require more *information;* it requires more *formation.*

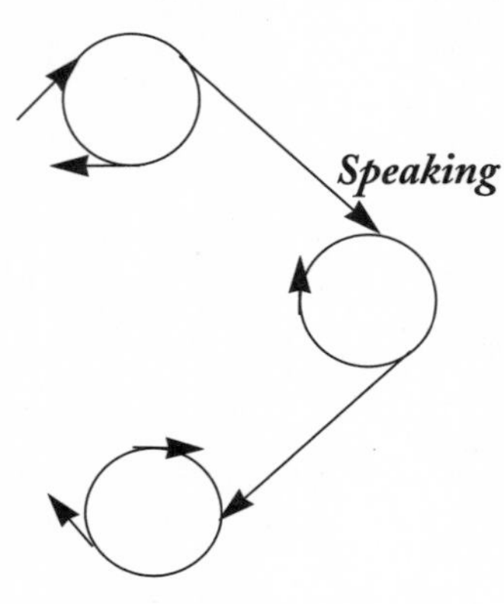

Adrian van Kaam distinguishes between approaching life in informative and formative ways.[8] The informative way is issue-oriented, logical, linear, and practical. Concerned with gaining clear answers to certain problems, it is detached and analytical. A mechanic uses informational thinking to figure out a car's problem; a shopper makes a list of what to buy at the grocery store; and a marital therapist analyzes information about a couple's communication patterns to determine the nature of their problems.

In contrast, the formative way is more reflective and meditative, focusing on our receptivity to how God is speaking to us through events, immediate situations, others, the world, and our hearts. When we approach life in a more formative way, we focus less on solving problems and more on discovering how God seeks to form, transform, and reform us. In effect, formative thinking allows us to listen more formatively for God in everything.

How often do you listen to the world in a reflective and meditative manner?

In what ways can you listen formatively in your life?

Take time to reflect on this.

As we rest in the listening cycle of prayer, we try to be more attentive to what God is calling us to do throughout life in general and in the more specific moments of life. People who listen for God in prayer attempt to listen to God when they discipline their children, when they offer advice to a friend, when they search for answers to a vexing situation in a business meeting, and when they wonder how to treat a homeless person asking for money. They are able to listen prayerfully to God even in the midst of life's busy moments.

When we listen to God, we do not ignore information; we just ensure that all information serves God's call and not our own desires—that it serves to *form* our lives. Listening to God is a filtering process; we retain information that helps us better understand God's call for us in that instance. This selective listening is difficult to do, especially in a culture that praises information gathering and treats it as an end in itself.

When we listen to God, we emphasize *wisdom* instead of *knowledge.* Wisdom is the art of understanding how to live, while knowledge is simply the gathering of facts, figures, and information. Gaining information leads to knowing things, but listening openly to God leads us to become wise. A prayer form like meditation can deepen our skill in listening to God and becoming wise. By quieting the world around us and asking for God's guidance with an open heart, we eventually can sense God's call in the silence. Meditation needs to go beyond formal periods of sitting in silent reflection. Every moment of life can be a moment of reflection and meditation in which we listen for God. We have to be willing to quiet our hearts on a constant basis, not just during those times when we decide to sit and meditate in silence for twenty or thirty minutes. We can seek to hear God's voice during even the most hectic moments. All we need are a desire and a willingness to listen to the quiet of our hearts.

What helps you listen to God through the daily events of your life?

As in the other cycles of praying, we can get stuck in this mode of prayer too. We can become overly rigid in our listening. While we may believe we are listening to God, we can easily substitute our own expectations for how God should respond and thereby close ourselves off to God.

I heard a story that illustrated this point well. A pastor was developing a sermon on the need to trust God. While working in his study, through the window he heard someone yelling, "The dam has burst! The dam has burst!" At first the frightened pastor started to run out the door to join the panic, but then he had an idea: *This will be a wonderful opportunity for me to practice what I preach. I'll wait here and trust God to save me.*

As the pastor waited for God to save him, the flood waters began to rise. A man paddled by in a small canoe as the pastor looked out of his second-floor window. "Jump in! I'll take you to safety," the man said. The pastor calmly responded, "No. Don't worry. God will save me." Soon the waters began to rise above the second floor. The pastor climbed into the attic and waited for God. A man in a motorboat came by and yelled to the pastor, "Here, get in and I'll get you out of here." The pastor said, "No, no. God will save me." Eventually the waters rose so high that the pastor had to climb out onto the roof. He waited there patiently as the waters surged around his ankles. A helicopter flew by, and the pilot yelled down, "Grab the ladder! We'll carry you to safety!" The pastor yelled back, "God will save me! Go on and don't worry." Soon the waters rose above the pastor's head, and he drowned.

The pastor found himself in heaven before God. "What happened, God?" he asked. "You were supposed to save me. I trusted you." God answered, "I sent you a canoe, a motorboat, and a helicopter. What else did you want?"

This story reflects how we stubbornly substitute our expectations for God's voice. Listening to God often means laying aside our expectations so that we can become more open to what God actually is saying to us, not what we want God to say. God usually does not speak through our limited language. God engages our imagination by speaking through symbols, relationships, events, the words of a book, and nature. Grounding ourselves in a religious tradition and community can help us distinguish God's voice from the compelling and confusing sounds of everyday life. Like Elijah, who listened to the silence while ignoring the tremendous sounds that we would expect to reflect God, we have to be willing to put aside our demand that God use only the voice we want to hear. We have to be willing to hear God as God calls us through every event of life.

How can you begin to emphasize wisdom over knowledge in your life?

Take time to ask God and to listen for God's response.

Loving Presence Cycle

Near the middle of the seventeenth century, a little-known French Carmelite monk named Brother Lawrence of the Resurrection was eulogized. We might never have heard about this monk at all were it not for Abbé de Beaufort's eulogy of Brother Lawrence. The Abbé de Beaufort described Brother Lawrence as an incredible man who had little talent for anything other than "living in the presence of God." Brother Lawrence's spiritual depth touched so many people that the Abbé de Beaufort made copies of his eulogy available, along with copies of some of Brother Lawrence's letters.

Brother Lawrence knew how to open his life to God's presence in every moment of life. Moment by moment, Brother Lawrence practiced what he called "the presence of God." Whatever he did, whether buying wine for the monastery or working in the kitchen, he made God an intimate part of his daily routine. As he said, "I cannot understand how a person in a religious community can live happily without the practice of the presence of God. As for me, I keep myself at rest with [God] at the depth and center of my soul as much as I can, and when I am with [God] in this way, I am not afraid of anything. But if I turn away from God even slightly, it is like Hell to me."[9]

Read 1 Thessalonians 5:17.

How do you relate this verse to Brother Lawrence's words?

How do you live in God's presence in your daily life?

Brother Lawrence's practice of inviting God into the most mundane moments of life is not only for monks. Each of us can do this, no matter what our vocation. When we invite God into every moment of life, we enter the *loving presence* cycle of prayer. In this prayer cycle, we move beyond thinking, speaking, and listening to God. We also allow ourselves to live continually with God in love and joy. When we go beyond listening to God and immerse ourselves in God's loving presence, we live with God moment by moment in our hearts. As Brother Lawrence put it, "We do not have to be constantly in church to be with God. We can make our heart a prayer room into which we can retire from time to time to converse with [God] gently, humbly and lovingly. Everyone is capable of these familiar conversations with God—some more, some less."[10]

Our awareness of God's loving presence sensitizes us to God's presence in everything. This cycle of praying integrates and incorporates all the other cycles. Thinking, speaking, and listening become ongoing activities. It can be more formal, such as the practice of contemplative prayer—a prayer form that emphasizes silence and resting with God with no agenda other than being with God. It can also be less structured and more spontaneous.

This kind of prayer is an incredibly open form of prayer. It opens us to appreciate God's presence at work, in the car, at the grocery store, in our child's soccer game, at the beach, in the woods, in front of the television, in the shower, when eating a meal with friends, or in the midst of any activity. Adopting this kind of prayer in our lives is difficult because of our ambivalence about how much we want God to be around. We may want God around in times of trouble, but we often bring God into the rest of our lives reluctantly. A church board member's comment reflects this dichotomy. He said that making decisions for a church was much harder than making decisions at work because in the church we have to worry about what God wants. The truth is that we need to care about what God wants wherever we are—to be willing to let God be a part of our jobs, our homes, and everything else too.

The truth is that we need to care about what God wants wherever we are—to be willing to let God be a part of our jobs, our homes, and everything else too.

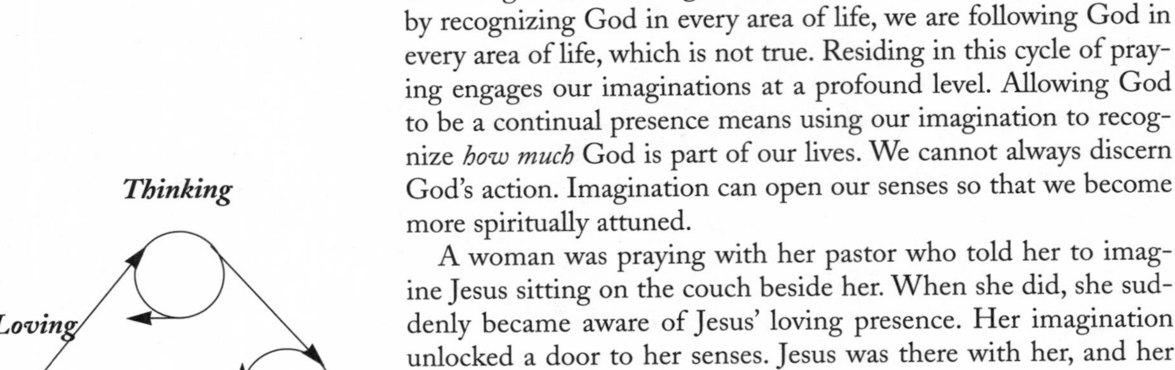

One danger of the loving presence cycle of praying rests in our confusing our own thoughts with God's call. We may assume that by recognizing God in every area of life, we are following God in every area of life, which is not true. Residing in this cycle of praying engages our imaginations at a profound level. Allowing God to be a continual presence means using our imagination to recognize *how much* God is part of our lives. We cannot always discern God's action. Imagination can open our senses so that we become more spiritually attuned.

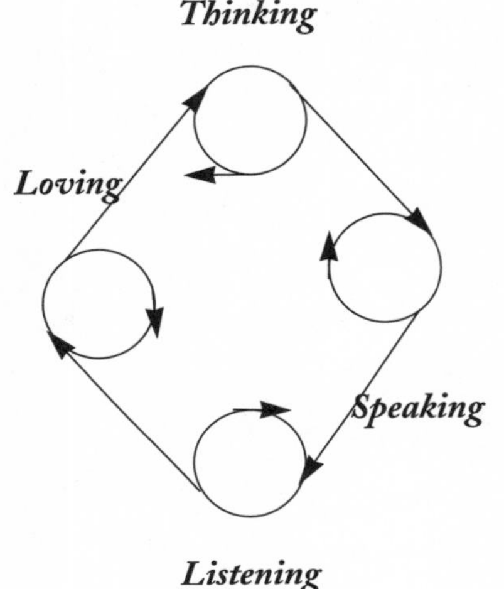

A woman was praying with her pastor who told her to imagine Jesus sitting on the couch beside her. When she did, she suddenly became aware of Jesus' loving presence. Her imagination unlocked a door to her senses. Jesus was there with her, and her imagination enabled her to sense his presence.

While our imagination can unlock a door to our senses, it can also take over our appreciation of God's presence. Instead of unlocking a door for Christ to enter, we can manufacture a Christ who will tell us only what we want to hear. We always must temper our imagination with reality. Many well-known television evangelists have run into trouble by confusing a manufactured presence for God's real presence, thereby closing themselves off to God.

We move into the loving presence cycle of prayer by continually opening our lives to God's will and by inviting God into every area of our lives. With this invitation, we naturally integrate all the cycles of praying into a larger cycle. By inviting God to be a constant presence, we deepen our prayer life as we deepen our faith. In this way, we naturally move back to the thinking cycle of prayer. Each time we do, our thoughts about God are enhanced. Our theologies and ideas about God expand because we have come to know God on a more personal level. Our thoughts reflect the fact that our love for God has deepened.

The Cycle of Prayer and Community

Remember that embracing the different cycles of praying can open us to following God. We must incorporate each cycle into the others. Calling each way of praying a cycle helps us remember that one cycle does not get rid of or supersede the others. Instead, the cycles interconnect. The different cycles complement one another and make up the whole realm of prayer.

Each cycle of praying goes beyond the personal dimension to the communal. As a church, community, or group, we can become stuck in a thinking, speaking, listening, or loving presence cycle of relating with God. In addition, each cycle is both an interior movement and an exterior action. As an individual or a church, we can become guilty of adopting a mission focus that we may *think* is right; yet because we never ask God for guidance, our mission does not serve God. We may move to a speaking cycle and *ask* God to support us in our outreach to others; yet because we never actually listen for God's call, our outreach may be misguided. We also may move to a listening cycle and actually *accept* and experience some success in a ministry that God calls us to. But unless we invite God's continued presence, our ministry can become self-serving and even destructive. Finally, as an individual or a church, we can *look* for God's continual presence in our ministry; yet over time success can cause us to think less critically about our ministry, to quit genuinely calling on God to act in our ministry, and to quit listening for God in our ministry. As a result we become arrogant in our assumption that God's presence with us justifies everything and makes it right. We enhance every cycle of prayer when we integrate the preceding and pursuant cycles. Each cycle of prayer is both individual and communal, involving interior reflection and exterior action.

How much do you invite God into every moment of your life?

Reflect on ways that you can allow God to be a greater presence.

When we move into the different cycles while integrating the other cycles, we deepen our faith and move closer to God, our source and our aim. As Paul Tillich writes, "Every prayer—with or without words—that reaches its aim, namely the reunion with the divine Ground of our being, is a work of the Spirit speaking in us and through us. Prayer is the Spiritual longing of a finite being to return to its origin."[11]

Prayer moves us along our journey toward God by helping us recognize and perceive God with more depth. Prayer, as the dialogue between ourselves and God, helps us understand more clearly what God seeks for us. It helps us articulate more clearly how we want God to touch our lives. It helps us listen more attentively to how God guides our lives. Finally, it helps us sense more deeply God's continued presence in our lives. When we respond to God's initiative and deepen our faith through prayer, we discover how much God leads us on our journey of faith.

Five

Grace and Confession

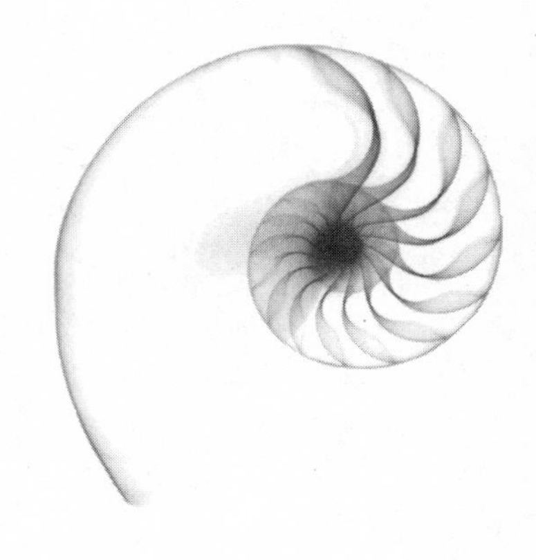

THEOLOGIAN JOHN B. COBB JR. wrote a poignant story about prayer and God's presence in the life of four young adults. The story describes how three friends of a young woman (Jennifer) in a comatose state try to help her as she slowly recovers from a car accident.[1] David, Janice, and Bill survive the accident; but as Jennifer slips closer to death, they become more and more distressed. It frustrates them to watch their friend die, and they sit by, helpless to do anything. Hope slowly fades as even the doctors seem powerless to help Jennifer. Finally one of the nurses tells Jennifer's friends that there is nothing left to do but pray. This suggestion gives David an idea—perhaps they can begin praying together for Jennifer. If prayer is all that's left, then maybe prayer is an answer.

So the friends gather together and pray for Jennifer. The next day an amazing thing happens. Jennifer's breathing, which had been labored and difficult, gradually becomes smoother and more fluid. An excited nurse tells Janice and David, "The doctors were wrong. Yesterday evening she turned some kind of corner. Sometimes it happens. We don't understand it; we just give thanks."[2] As the days pass, the three friends gather to pray more often, and Jennifer improves gradually. Eventually Jennifer comes out of her coma and begins the long process of rehabilitation.

Despite her improvement, Jennifer is no longer the same person. Her memory has become fragmented, and her personality has changed dramatically. While she had always been kind and friendly, she is now increasingly petulant and irritable. It is not easy to be around her, and the friends realize there will be little improvement in the future. Jennifer will never be able to return to school or to be a normal companion to people her own age. If

God wanted to heal her, why didn't God restore her to the way she had been? It is all so unfair.

Jennifer's friends pray even harder:

> They pleaded with God. They made great promises of what they would do if God would fully heal her. Sometimes they expressed their anger with God. Nothing seemed to make any difference. Had God played a trick on them, encouraging them and then stopping with results that were ambiguous indeed? Jennifer was an unhappy child in a young woman's body, a child without prospects of ever growing up. Was this better than the death that had once seemed so imminent?[3]

The three friends continue to struggle to understand God's work in Jennifer's life with all its unpredictability and inconsistency. They never receive adequate answers—only silence. They are left to wonder, *Why, God? Why?* The friends agree to keep praying for Jennifer despite their doubts. They thank God for what God has done so far, and they ask for the strength to remain supportive of Jennifer. Jennifer never fully recovers. Cobb's story leaves us grappling with our questions about how, why, where, and in what way God is involved in our lives.

Do you struggle with the closeness or distance of God in your life?

At what times does God seem distant?

Reflect on these questions, and consider your current experience of God.

The Distant God

This story's lack of resolution disturbs us. Yet, as Christians, we struggle to determine whether or not God truly is active in this world, and we struggle to discern how God is active. At times God seems tremendously distant—especially when we witness or experience prolonged pain and suffering. We call out to God and ask, "Why?" This distant and uninvolved God shakes our faith. We wonder why God relates to us in this way.

At other times, God may seem unexpectedly close to us. David, Janice, and Bill perceived God's nearness and activity in Jennifer's initial emergence from the coma. Many of us also may sense God's intimate presence at a wedding, the birth of a child, the funeral of a loved one, a new and unexpected job offer, a friend's listening deeply to our troubles, a sudden upward turn for our lives. Why does God seem so close at these points of life, and yet so distant at others? Perhaps a look at how the earliest Christians experienced God might help us.

The Intimate God of Grace

The earliest Christians who gathered together on Pentecost and who formed the first churches believed in God as an intimate, caring, and tangible presence who gives humans the freedom to choose their own course in life. They understood God as surrounding us, yet offering each person the choice of being open to God. These Christians also understood that ultimately God chooses whether or not to act in our lives. We cannot make God do anything. God chooses to act in our lives and does so by blessing us with God's *grace*—a mysterious force that affects our lives and all of life in many ways. God's grace is God's power working major and minor miracles throughout our lives. We experience the effects of God's grace whenever God influences the events of our lives, yet we also experience God's grace whenever God lets us determine how we will live our lives.

God's *active grace* (those events in which God's presence seems clear) is easy for us to accept; God's quiet and *silent grace* (those events in which God's presence is hard to discern) causes turmoil in our lives. Jennifer's friends easily accepted the active grace of God's immediate healing. They had trouble accepting the silent grace of the ensuing recovery as Jennifer struggled to regain the life she had lost. They wanted God to act in ways they could easily recognize and understand, rather than in the silent and more subtle ways. Understandably, they expected God to act according to their demands and desires. They had a vision for Jennifer's healing, and they expected God to abide by that vision.

In what ways do you let God's grace work in your life?

In what ways do you inhibit God's grace?

Take time to consider how both approaches serve as indicators of God's grace at work in your life.

What David, Janice, and Bill did not expect or realize was that even in their exclusive focus on Jennifer, God's grace was mysteriously at work, actively nurturing a deeper faith in them. An awareness of God's presence in every area of life began to develop within them—God was present with Jennifer and with them.

God's grace (at least from our perspective) is always greater and more dynamic than we expect. We expect it to apply to certain areas of life and not others. We pray for others, expecting God to heal them, not us. We fail to appreciate God's concern with the transformation and healing of whole world.

God's Great Grace

Basically we do not appreciate the greatness of God's grace. We do not appreciate the fact that grace and freedom of choice go hand in hand. As we discussed in chapter two, sometimes we make the mistake of assuming that because our perception of God's grace is most attuned in times of crisis, God must have caused the crisis. Why else would bad things happen to us?

It must be a test. Many preachers and well-known devotional writers have based their ministries upon this belief. They say that God causes life's difficulties as a test to demonstrate the depths of God's grace. They assert that everything is the way it should be and that nothing happens by accident. If something bad happens, well, it must be God's will. This outlook makes God seem manipulative or cruel.

How sensitive to God's presence are you?

Do you sense God only in certain events of life or in many?

Take time to pray to God for increased sensitivity to God's grace.

We might do better to recognize that daily life offers many opportunities for God to act, and God does. The freedom that God gives us—that God gives the whole universe—to interact creates dynamic possibilities that human beings cannot control. God brings new possibilities to life, especially when all hope is gone. This is how God works. God spreads grace throughout life so that, despite the dangers of life, God can lead us to new life. God does not have to create situations for grace. They abound.

In a passage from John's Gospel, Jesus comes upon a man who has been blind from birth. Immediately his disciples ask, "Rabbi, who sinned, this man or his parents, that he was born blind?" (John 9:2) Their question arose out of a common belief of the time that persists today: the belief that physical deformity and disease directly result from sin—either one's ancestors' or one's own. This belief offered clear answers to people struggling to understand God's ways. Good health and wealth evidenced a person's moral character, while lack of health and wealth signified immorality or spiritual debasement.

Try to remember those times in which you have experienced God's grace in your lives.

What made you more sensitive?

Jesus responds with an alternative: "Neither this man nor his parents sinned; he was born blind so that God's works might be revealed in him" (John 9:3). That is not the kind of answer that Jesus' disciples expected. Many Christians have struggled with this answer because it sounds as though God cruelly causes deformity, turmoil, pain, and suffering just to receive glory when relief comes. But Jesus' answer faults no one. This was a radical thought for Jesus' day. Jesus goes further, saying that crippling disease, misfortune, and suffering provide opportunities for us to discover God—to witness God's grace in physical, relational, and spiritual healing. Evidence of God's grace lies in Jesus' restoring the man's sight.

Grace is both apparent and mysterious, active and silent. The term *grace* literally means blessing, favor, and approval. We do not deserve God's gift of grace. We receive God's grace because God loves us so much that God wants to bless and favor our lives. According to Paul, Jesus embodied grace and made it available to all (Rom. 5:15-18). John Calvin assures us that grace has been present since Creation: "After realizing that there is a Creator, it must then infer that he is also Governor and Preserver, not just because he can produce a kind of general motion in the machine of the universe, as well as in each of its parts, but because by his special Providence he sustains and cares for everything he has made down to the smallest sparrow!"[4]

God's grace is God's undying commitment to each and every one of us.

God's grace is God's undying commitment to each and every one of us. God recognizes our weakness in the face of life. We grapple with many demands: How shall we conduct our business life? How stringently or loosely shall we discipline our children? How far does our commitment to a spouse go? How much of our time and money shall we devote to the poor and disadvantaged? Does it really matter if we worship God?

The list of demands and concerns goes on and on. God's grace as a gift of strength helps us face these demands. As John Macquarrie states, "Grace is first and foremost a gift, and in its most typical form, it is the self-giving of a person. God's grace is simply [God's] self-giving, self-bestowing, self-commitment, in... acts of creation and redemption."[5] We enhance this gift of grace whenever we open ourselves to God and God's grace.

When you have experienced God's grace, did it come as an unexpected gift from God, or do you feel as though you "obtained" it somehow?

Take time to reflect on this.

Despite the assurance of God's gift of grace that surrounds us, we still have questions: Why do we so often feel that God is distant and aloof? Part of the answer may reside in the mysterious, subtle, and unpredictable nature of God's grace. How can we understand the ways of grace when they remain undetectable? Let me offer a metaphor that may help.

Growing up in Pittsburgh, Pennsylvania, I watched the Pittsburgh Steelers on a weekly basis during the years when they won four Super Bowls in six years. I took real pleasure in watching Terry Bradshaw, the Steelers' quarterback, throw the football to his two great receivers Lynn Swann and John Stallworth. In many ways I see his passes as similar to God's grace (although, unlike many Pittsburghers at the time, I am unwilling to equate Bradshaw with God). Often, under heavy pressure, Bradshaw threw the ball to Swann or Stallworth as they ran to get open. Often

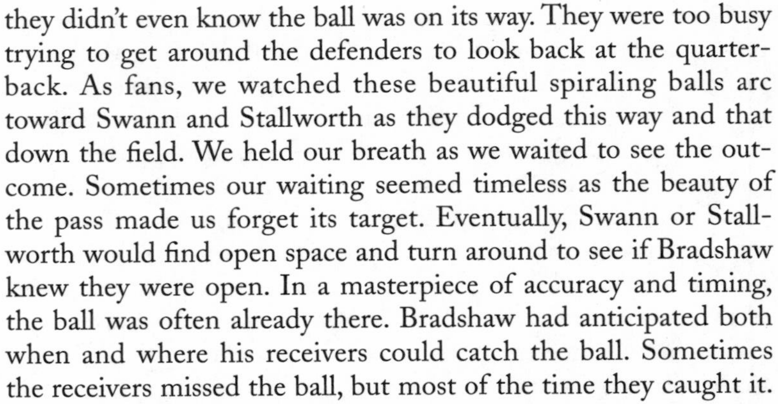

they didn't even know the ball was on its way. They were too busy trying to get around the defenders to look back at the quarterback. As fans, we watched these beautiful spiraling balls arc toward Swann and Stallworth as they dodged this way and that down the field. We held our breath as we waited to see the outcome. Sometimes our waiting seemed timeless as the beauty of the pass made us forget its target. Eventually, Swann or Stallworth would find open space and turn around to see if Bradshaw knew they were open. In a masterpiece of accuracy and timing, the ball was often already there. Bradshaw had anticipated both when and where his receivers could catch the ball. Sometimes the receivers missed the ball, but most of the time they caught it.

Reflect on your life.

When has God acted in ways that were so subtle you thought God was absent, but later you discovered God's presence?

Take time to thank God for these times.

God sends grace our way in beautiful arcs, yet we often are unaware of the fact. We focus our lives on immediate events, while wondering if God will ever help us. Meanwhile God influences events beyond our awareness, and the consequences speed toward us. God's grace is most amazing at those moments when we turn around and discover that God has already acted. We tend to recognize God's grace only when clearly visible and apparent. Much of the time, we do not see God's grace at work and remain ignorant of the depth of God's touch on our lives.

Even when we miss God's grace, God willingly sends more grace our way. Perhaps our sense of God's distance and aloofness indicates our lack of awareness of how God is working outside our fields of perception. Sometimes specific passes of grace can take weeks, months, and even years to reach us.

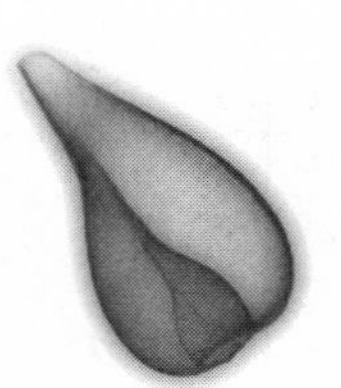

Our Distance from God

Another reason God often seems so distant and aloof has to do with human nature. As much as we would prefer not to recognize it, we have a strong tendency to push God away and to refuse to accept God's grace because of our sin. We want to control our lives, and yet truly accepting God's grace requires us to give up control of our lives. Our sinful tendency to push God away hinders us from receiving God's grace.

I once talked with another minister about sin and our spiritual need for awareness of sin's power in our lives. The minister remarked, "I don't want to hear about sin. The idea of sin has done more damage to us over time than anything else. I think it's a bunch of crap!" He had a point. In the past, the church has focused so much on sin that people have walked around feeling guilty for no justifiable reason. Many domineering clergy have used the concept of sin to manipulate and control people. Manipulative parents exercise this concept to make their children more compliant and obedient. Sin has been one of the most abused religious concepts in Christianity's history. We have become so wary of the sinful abuses of the concept of sin that we have exiled it from many of our churches. Some churches have deleted confession from their services altogether as a way of downplaying sin. Many older theologians, ministers, and priests wonder aloud, "Whatever became of sin?"

We have a choice: Will we let sin rule our lives or let God rule our lives?

Have we overreacted to these abuses by denying the reality of sin? Cognizance of our sin should not occasion feelings of guilt and depression. Sin is part of human nature, part of who we are. We often confuse human sin with the belief that human nature is awful and terrible. Sin may lead us to act in uncaring, abusive, and sometimes evil ways, but sin does not necessarily *make* us behave in these ways. We have a choice: Will we let sin rule our lives or let God rule our lives? Often we remain unaware of how we have chosen to let sin dominate our lives.

Let us look at the concept of sin in more detail. Paul Tillich's writings have done much to clarify the concept of sin and to rescue it from a simple identification with bad behavior and immoral activities. Tillich asserts that at its foundation, Sin (with a capital *S*) is *estrangement* from God, from others, and from ourselves; and this estrangement characterizes all of human existence.[6] He capitalized the word to distinguish the state of *Sin* from the act of *sin*. Because of our estrangement from God, we humans tend to separate and alienate ourselves from everything else in creation. At times we dominate or reject others, criticize or idolize ourselves, destroy or worship nature, and minimize or reject God. While not the way we *should* live our lives, separation and alienation often characterize how we *do* live our lives.

By using the word *estrangement*, Tillich suggests that although we make ourselves strangers to God and God's ways, this is not how God wants us to be. God did not create us to be estranged from all of life—to be strangers to all that is good and that comes from God. God created us in love for love and relationship. Yet we choose to alienate ourselves from one another, from God, and from our own true nature and being.

We tend to define or describe a sin as any deviation from

moral law. This definition ignores the fact that Sin is primarily a power or force that alienates our lives.[7] Our emphasis on the moral nature of sin rather than the foundational nature of Sin can distract us. When we focus on sin, we tend to forget that *acts of sin* arise out of our *Sin*—our state of estrangement from God. Tillich says that sin implies "the personal act of turning away from that to which one belongs."[8] Whenever we engage in an act of sin, we turn from God; and we do so because of our Sin—because of our natural tendency to separate and alienate ourselves from God, others, and ourselves. Our failure to distinguish between Sin, the state of being, and sin, the act, has led to our abuse of the concept of sin.

We judge others for their sins—for their immoral behavior—while conveniently forgetting that our judgment of others for their sins fully expresses our own sinful nature. Whenever we judge others, we push away others as well as God. We notice the sins of others while remaining ignorant of the sinful nature that envelops us and keeps us from truly loving and caring about God and others. Thus, Sin restricts our relationship with God by provoking us to push God away.

We can detect the ravages of Sin easily. We sin on a personal level whenever we treat another person with a lack of respect or in an uncaring way. We also sin personally when we severely criticize ourselves for not being smarter, more competent, or better-liked. This criticism expresses our tendency to separate ourselves from God's love for us.

Sin is not only personal; it is *communal.* We demonstrate our sinful nature whenever we care *only* about a spotted owl or another endangered species or ecosystem, and not about people who struggle to make a living. We demonstrate Sin whenever we care *only* about people struggling to make a living and not about endangered species and ecosystems. Both of these cases express Sin because they emphasize separation and alienation by making one part of God's creation so important that it legitimizes the destruction or abuse of another part. Estrangement results whenever we selfishly determine that one group, species, or ecosystem is more important than others. Here our Sin expresses itself in our pushing away from God's call to live harmoniously as we emphasize one group, cause, or concern over others.

How do you understand the concept of sin?

Where are you most aware of sin in your life?

Take time to pray to God about this.

Sin also can be expressed on a global level. We discover the ravaging effects of Sin whenever one national, cultural, racial, or ethnic group discriminates or violates another; when one group makes itself more important than another and acts to oppress or control the other. Sin is one of the most evident dynamics of life. It finds expression in acts of racism, criticism, violence, indifference, destruction, isolation, anger, and domination. While we may not want to admit it, our sinful nature is responsible for our failure to live harmoniously and peaceably on personal, communal, and global levels. Whenever we choose to ignore, minimize, or avoid God's call and grace in our lives, acts of sin are the byproduct. Thus, we alienate ourselves from God's original grace that seeks expression in our lives. We cannot completely erase Sin's power in our lives. When we willingly recognize and admit its influence and power in our lives, we discover God revealing a way to move beyond it.

Reflect on your life. What are some of the small ways you separate yourself from God, others, and yourself?

Take time to pray to God about this.

Bridging the Abyss through Confession

When we ignore or avoid the reality of Sin in our lives, we also inhibit a powerful spiritual practice that actually weakens Sin's influence over our lives. While we may recognize the importance of prayer, study, worship, service, meditation, and even time spent in solitude, we often ignore the power of *confession*. Our inherent tendency to insulate ourselves from God, ourselves, and others often causes us to give up the practice of serious confession. We do not want to face up to our responsibility for the turmoil of our lives. We do not want to accept the separating dynamic that influences many of our actions. We would rather complain of God's distance, of others who have something against us, or of our troubles that arise from difficult childhoods. We do not like to face our own shadow side. Then we let Sin get in the way of our relationship with God.

I believe I became fully aware of the power of confession at age twenty-four. Nine years earlier, I had rejected Christianity and had decided to forge my own path. Church was not on that path. I did not necessarily reject God or even Christ, but I did reject institutional religion. Throughout college and into my work as a therapist in a psychiatric hospital, I followed my own psychologically based spiritual path. Psychology had become my religion, and counseling was my mission. Then at age twenty-four, I found myself embroiled in a personal, psychological, and spiritual crisis.

Read Genesis 2:8-25.

What does this passage say about how we are to live in relationship to God, nature, and one another?

For a variety of reasons, I had become disillusioned with the counseling profession, and all the books on psychology in the world could not show me the light. My faith in the theories of Freud, Jung, Skinner, and Erikson were shattered. I felt alone and unable to sense God in my life. My personal and professional frustrations led me to believe that God did not care about my fate. After a long, painful struggle with my individualistic pride, I decided to join a local church. I met with the pastor who asked me why I wanted to join. I was scared to tell him the truth—that I was not as independent and in control of my life as I thought I had been. In a surge of tears, I made my confession to him: "I just can't do it alone anymore. I can't search for God alone anymore. I've been trying to follow God for the past nine years all by myself, and I don't know where God is anymore. I can't live without the help of others. I need to be part of a group, a church which will help me find God. I used to think that the church was full of fake people who really didn't want to find God. Maybe it still is. Maybe it isn't. All I know is that I have to join a church so I can find God again."[9]

Amidst my sobs, I confessed to the pastor and to God that my independent search was a failure and that I needed God, the pastor, and the church to help me. This confession changed my life. Previously I had pushed God and others away by making my own independence and rebellion a special god of my own. Living my own way had become so important to me that I had alienated myself from most of the people, groups, and traditions that could have helped me form a deeper relationship with God. Only after making this confession was I ready to open myself to God's amazing grace. My whole life changed as I became less self-directed and more open to God's directives. I still struggle to follow God's ways, but now I am more open to possibilities.

How do you feel about confession?

Is it a practice you see as antiquated or as relevant?

Is it something you engage in regularly, or something that seems unnecessary and depressing?

Take time to reflect on this.

One of the greatest opportunities to open ourselves to God's grace emerges whenever we confess to God our Sin—whenever we confess to God how we have alienated ourselves from God, others, and ourselves. Sometimes this confession involves another person (a priest, a minister, or simply a spiritually mature person) who helps us clarify our thoughts and assures us of God's love. Most of the time we can offer our confessions directly to God.

Confession to God does not mean we need to name every naughty or bad thing we have ever done, nor do we need to focus on how terrible we are. An overly critical examination distracts us and can actually push God away. Self-examination becomes sinful when we refuse to accept God's grace and choose to wallow in excessive self-criticism. Confession should arise out of our *gentle* self-examination in which we uncover and discover how we have alienated ourselves from God. In confession we take responsibility for our failure to become the persons God created and calls us to be. We maturely face up to the fear, selfishness, and insecurity that generally cause us to make ambitions, activities, behaviors, and beliefs more important than God.

Confession is meant to liberate. Richard J. Foster expresses this idea beautifully when he states that there must come a point at which we give up our self-examination: "Otherwise, we can easily fall into a permanent habit of self-condemnation. Confession begins in sorrow, but it ends in joy. There is a celebration in the forgiveness of sins because it results in a genuinely changed life."[10]

Even on a purely psychological level, admission of responsibility is important. For instance, a crucial moment in counseling comes when we accept a reasonable amount of responsibility for the pain of our lives and admit this to the therapist. We might accept responsibility for harming another or for harming ourselves. We might accept responsibility for allowing past traumas and problems to continue ruining our lives. When we engage in this kind of psychological self-examination and admission, we discover freedom from the tyranny of our past.

Have you ever stubbornly clung to a belief or a lifestyle that you knew was destructive but could not change?

What caused things to change?

Was confession a part of it?

Take time to reflect on this.

Confession similarly liberates us on a spiritual level. Confession helps us let go of spiritual obstacles so we can accept God's love for us. This process of letting go of obstacles to God, while simultaneously accepting God, provides the basis for religious conversion. In Twelve-Step programs, persons' admission of powerlessness over life allows them to yield to a higher power or God—to let go and let God. Whenever we confess to God that we have pushed God away, we engage in a process of letting go of destructive lifestyles and attitudes so we can accept God's guidance and love. When we offer an honest confession to God, we let God tear down the walls with which we have surrounded ourselves—walls that may protect us from pain but that also keep us from experiencing God's grace. Confession is the first step in becoming more open to God's grace.

Confession is also a healing part of every relationship. Contrary to a popular phrase from the seventies ("love means never having to say you're sorry"), love means constantly having to say you're sorry. The two phrases "I'm sorry" and "I love you" do more to deepen relationships than anything else we can say. Unless both partners in a relationship willingly admit their faults and their mistakes, the relationship never matures. The unwillingness of one person to admit fault eventually creates a painful relationship. Love for another person only deepens when we are willing to admit fault, which is especially true in regard to our love for God. Admitting our fault (in a responsible and balanced way) helps us discover the depths of God's love for us.

Read Romans 8:31-39.

What do these verses suggest about God's response to your confessions?

In confessing Sin, we keep in mind our intention, which is to deepen our relationship with God. Once we confess, we let Sin go, trusting in God's love for us. Confession then is an act of letting go of all that alienates us from God. It opens us to the real beauty of Christian faith, which is that God does not hold our Sin against us. Most Christian traditions have a ritual of confession during the worship service. We offer our confession to God, and then we hear of God's love and forgiveness. Sometimes we affirm together, "In Jesus Christ we are forgiven. Thanks be to God!" Then we move on with the service. We do not linger on Sin. We move forward with the confidence that God loves us.

John's Gospel clearly depicts God's forgiving nature: "For God so loved the world that he gave his only Son, so that everyone who believes in him may not perish but may have eternal life. Indeed, God did not send the Son into the world to condemn the world, but in order that the world might be saved through him" (3:16-17). These verses make it clear that God does not focus on Sin, and therefore neither should we. God focuses on love, as should we.

Do you have a hard time admitting fault? Why?

Take time to examine your life and consider what aspects get in the way of confession.

Confession is a discipline and a ritual that helps us honestly and openly offer our lives to God in order to accept God's *grace*. The German theologian Dietrich Bonhoeffer expressed this sentiment beautifully when he wrote, "Now come, as the sinner you are, to God who loves you. [God] wants you as you are; [God] does not want anything from you, a sacrifice, a work; [God] wants you alone. 'My son [and daughter], give me thine heart' (Prov. 23:26). God has come to save the sinner. Be glad! This message is liberation through truth."[11] Accepting God's love avails us of the powerful grace in which our lives are grounded.

Accepting this deep grace requires responsible action. Bonhoeffer suggests that we often try to procure a cheap version of

God's grace. We want good from God without our willingness to enter into a deep and responsible relationship to receive it. He says that the cheap grace we often try to get is

> the preaching of forgiveness without requiring repentance, baptism without church discipline, Communion without confession, absolution without personal confession. Cheap grace is grace without discipleship, grace without the cross, grace without Jesus Christ, living and incarnate. . . .
>
> Costly grace is the gospel which must be *sought* again and again, the gift which must be *asked* for, the door at which [we] must *knock*.[12]

When we seek the mature grace and love of God, then we reconnect with who we are; and we open ourselves in a deep way to becoming the people God wants us to be. We become open to God's transforming love, and transformation of lives is the ministry of Christ yesterday, today, and tomorrow.

Take time to look at ways you push God away.

Confess these to God, and seek God's forgiveness and healing.

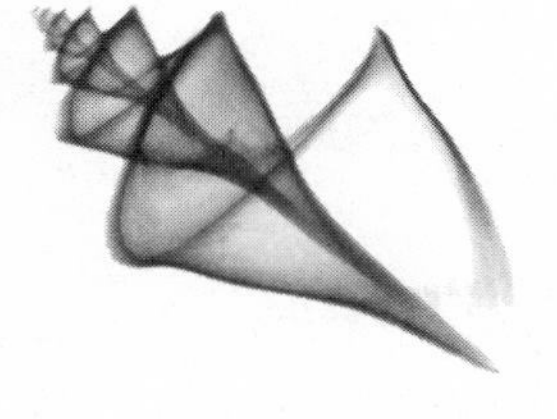

Six

Commitment and Community

SEVERAL YEARS AGO I had dinner with some friends at a very good restaurant. As we ate, our conversation deftly moved from topic to topic. We explored topics such as great North American cities, the worst songs of all time, and an upcoming wedding. Eventually we moved on to the subject of faith and church. One of my companions made a piercing comment: "I don't see why it's so important to go to church. I think we can be spiritual whether we go to church or not. You know, every time I go to church, I die of boredom. I always sit there wondering what this is doing for me. I get more inspiration from going out into a field or reading a great poem."

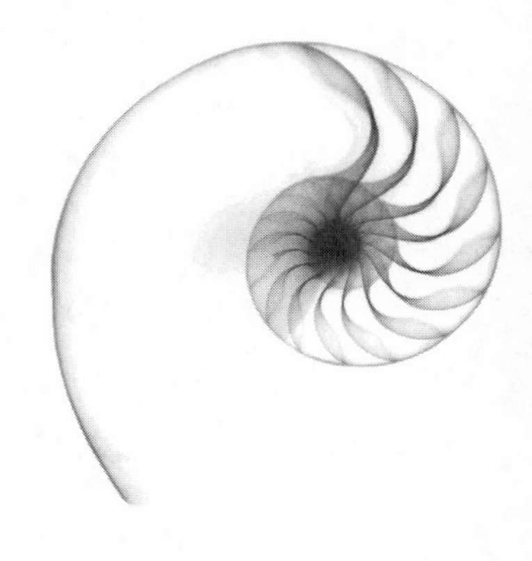

She had a good point, and one that we hear not only throughout our culture but throughout the world. Can we be spiritual without going to church? Not long ago this kind of thought would have shocked people. Until the eighteenth century, people in Western civilizations were immersed in a culture that took church membership for granted. Prior to the eighteenth century, most Westerners had no concept of a life that did not revolve around religion and the church. Spiritual growth and the church went hand in hand.[1] Participation in church traditions and rituals provided opportunities for reconciliation and communion with God in Christ.

Can we be spiritual without going to church?

Over the past few centuries, the emergence of rational and scientific thinking has changed our perceptions. Increased emphasis on independent thought and personal experience has affected our religious pursuits. In stark contrast to most religious seekers of the seventeenth, eighteenth, and nineteenth centuries, many of today's spiritual seekers believe that church participation actually hinders spiritual growth.

My dinner companion exemplified the way many people view the church: The church is irrelevant and boring. In my younger days, I too believed that while sometimes church participation fostered spiritual growth, it was better to "go it alone." As a friend once said, "All the churches I've been to are so dull. The priests are so dry and out of touch, and it always seems like there's a gap between them and us. I just can't think going to church does me any good. I'd rather find God on my own." In some ways, this solo approach makes sense. If God really is calling each of us to individual faith journeys, then maybe we should break free from *all* religious systems—especially churches that seem so repressive, patriarchal, archaic, and out of touch.

As a woman and I walked and talked together on a beautiful summer day, she told me that she disliked churches because they made her feel guilty. She commented that "all this talk about sin just tries to make me feel guilty. It reflects the patriarchal nature of Christianity and especially of the Bible. They use sin to keep people like me down, and I say this as a person who was a little 'church-kid' as a child." This woman understood church as part of a system that prevented her from discovering how God's image is expressed through her individuality.

Spiritual Individualism

The opinions voiced above indicate a desire to break free of repressive religious systems to follow God in one's own way. By seeking God on their own, these people believe they can discover God as God really is rather than as Christianity presents God. I remember commenting to a friend in college: "Christianity only gets in my way. It keeps me from discovering who God really is." I meant it too. However, in my rejection of all religious systems in favor of my independent pursuit, I substituted a quasi-religious belief that can do great spiritual damage: the belief that only I, as an individual, am qualified to determine the validity of my own spiritual path.

Read Matthew 18:20.

What does this passage say about individualistic faith?

Read Luke 4:16.

If Jesus serves as our example of faith, how greatly do you think he valued worshiping with others?

As an independent spiritual person, I believed that I did not need the guidance and help of religious people and religious traditions. *Spiritual individualism* praises independent spiritual practices and pursuits, while criticizing the flaws of communal approaches—especially those that are part of established religious traditions. The beliefs of spiritual "do it yourselfers" do not recognize the importance of spiritual communities like churches. While individual spirituality is important, we need to balance it with communal spirituality, or it may lead to spiritual narcissism—a spiritual self-centeredness and egotism.

The emphasis on individual spirituality arises out of a greater tradition of *individualism.* As a cultural tradition, individualism teaches us that all life revolves around us as individuals; we must be self-reliant. In the book *Habits of the Heart,* sociologist Robert N. Bellah and his colleagues presented a groundbreaking study on America's fascination with the individual.[2] They see individualism as a part of American culture and history. Because people seeking personal and religious freedom colonized America, many of the original colonists—especially the Puritans—stressed a need for personal religious experience. Individual thought and expression became an important part of life in the American colonies. America became the place to pursue individual ideals. As America gained its independence and began to develop its own stories and mythology, this individualistic ideal was expressed more often. Eventually, as Bellah and his colleagues note, individualism developed into a national ideal:

> To serve society, one must be able to stand alone, not needing others, not depending on their judgment, and not submitting to their wishes. Yet this individualism is not selfishness. Indeed, it is a kind of heroic selflessness. One accepts the necessity of remaining alone in order to serve the values of the group.[3]

This American ideal of individualism has resulted in the zealous pursuit of self-reliance, especially among men. Women seem more immune to the emphasis on being an individual, although this may be changing too as women become more competitive with men. The emphasis on individuality causes us to become overly independent, if not in reality, then at least in our imaginations. The pursuit of self-reliance has led many of us to try to create our own personal, moral, and spiritual foundations. By becoming self-reliant, we hope to take charge of our own lives and to blaze trails that lead to personal sources of meaning. As Bellah and his colleagues state, "Clearly, the meaning of one's life for most Americans is to become one's own person, almost to give birth to oneself."[4]

Many of the problems that plague our society have emerged from this emphasis on individualism.

Many of the problems that plague our society have emerged

Reflect on your own faith.

Do you tend to see your own faith as personal and private, or do you see it as something to be shared with others?

from this emphasis on individualism. Individualism can cause people selfishly to pursue their own desires while ignoring the good of the greater community. When individualism becomes too strong, it breaks down our ability to work together in community. The self-reliant person feels pressured to be independent and not to conform, even in the face of a need to cooperate. Becoming too much our own person can cause us to ignore the guiding and nurturing power of community.

Leo N. Miletich laments the loss of manners in our present culture as a result of the power of individualism. He writes of the behavioral changes he has noticed among people living in apartments. He suggests that overall, people have become ruder:

> Some neighbors use car horns in lieu of doorbells; other residents have barking dogs. A number of people can't seem to hear music unless the beat is vibrating the walls and rattling the windows; and there are those dysfunctional couples who debate by smashing crockery against the walls.... There are helpful souls who keep their televisions so loud that I have no need to use the sound on mine if we're on the same channel.[5]

These experiences differ from his childhood experiences in which consideration for others was part of the communal, neighborhood life. In our present culture, imposing loudly on others has become common behavior, and it reflects our individualism. Too often we only care about our own desires and concerns, while ignoring the welfare of those around us. We also tend to ignore the impact that such extreme self-focus has on our own lives. Extreme individualism hurts us on social, psychological, and spiritual levels.

Spiritual individualism makes us spiritual water spiders skimming across the surface of many different traditions.

When we become spiritually individualistic, we tend to make ourselves the center of all religious and spiritual appraisal. In other words, when I become spiritually individualistic, I tend to see all religious systems and traditions as relative. I adopt the belief that I am the only person fit to judge the healthiness of a particular spiritual practice or religious ideal. Spiritual individualism makes us spiritual water spiders skimming across the surface of many different traditions. We pick and choose from each, but we never move deeply enough into one particular tradition to discover the depth and wisdom that it offers.

Worshiping God Substitutes

Great spiritual mystics understand the secret of spiritual growth: We have to sink our roots deeply into a religious tradition that teaches us how to pray, to listen for God's voice, and to live our lives. The great mystics have always been people who are deeply nourished by their religious traditions, even though they sometimes have had to reform these traditions to rid them of their destructive elements. The great mystics do not seek their own way. They seek the pathways that the mystics who came before them have set. Churches hand down the ways of the mystics, but we have to delve deeply to discover these ways.

Often we assume that God wants what we want, but our wants are not always spiritually nourishing.

Spiritual individualism often leads to one of two pitfalls. First, we make ourselves independent spiritual experts. We may try to create God in our image, expecting God to fulfill our narrow expectations. This endeavor keeps us from discovering the true God who is more than we expect—who is a deep and wonderful mystery. Instead, we may create in our minds a personal genie, a god who wants nothing more than to satisfy our personal desires and wishes.

Often we assume that God wants what we want, but our wants are not always spiritually nourishing. They can actually become spiritually destructive, and creating God in our own image only exacerbates our own destructive tendencies.

What kinds of things might be God substitutes in your life?

Take time in prayer to talk with God about this.

Ask God to open you more to God as God really is.

Spiritual individualism can cause us to create God in our own image, and it can lead to a second pitfall: *God substitutes.* Spiritual individualism can lead us to substitute things for God. This often happens in our culture. While originally we may have had noble thoughts about pursuing God alone, we easily become obsessed with God substitutes. Anything can become a God substitute. We can slavishly pursue wealth, power, exercise, sexual expression and experimentation, music, art, ideas, drugs and alcohol, isolation, spiritual experimentation, relationships, or sports. Too much independence can foster practices that become substitutes for the God we have ignored.

The tendency to create God substitutes arises as a result of the spiritual yearning within each of us. We all yearn for the transcendent—that which is beyond us—yet whenever we ignore healthy and enriching spiritual outlets for this yearning, it finds other outlets. A person devoted to sports may become obsessed with winning at the expense of relationships, career, and health. The person devoted to business may seek more money and influence, while ignoring the welfare of others. The person devoted to exercise can become consumed with getting in perfect shape at the expense of personal relationships. When we focus all of our energies on these activities, they can become substitutes for God. In the process we either repress or co-opt our spiritual yearnings.

We are unique as individuals only because God created us and endowed us with certain gifts that reflect God's image.

Uniqueness Rather Than Individualism

While spiritual individualism can become a problem, we do not avoid it by denying the importance of the individual or individual pursuits or by demanding that we engage only in the more communal approaches. Such solutions deny our personal *individuality* and *uniqueness*. Recognizing our own distinctiveness and uniqueness is an important part of our spiritual growth. Yet a difference exists between individualism and individuality. Personal individualism is an attempt to create ourselves in isolation from God—to be the complete masters of our lives, to be in complete control. True individuality arises out of our uniqueness, our being a personal expression of the image of God.[6] Most of us do not appreciate this fact, but *we are unique as individuals only because God created us and endowed us with certain gifts that reflect God's image.* What we do does not make us special; our uniqueness comes in our becoming the people God created us to be. As true individuals, our purpose in life is to express God uniquely through our talents, abilities, and actions. Our purpose is not necessarily the attainment of personal goals and desires. God created us as unique expressions of God's love, will, and purpose, which we express only when we follow our calling.

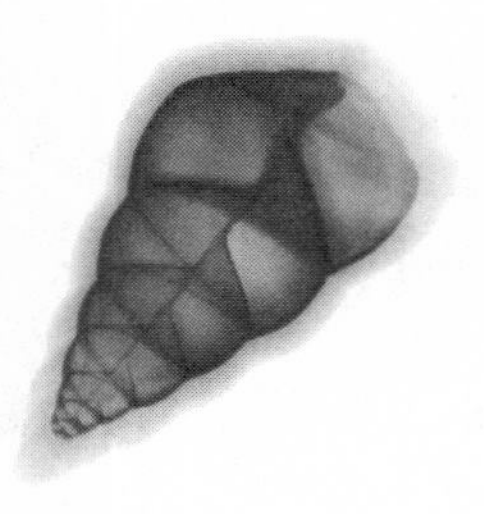

Jesus speaks about our uniqueness in the parable of the talents from Matthew's Gospel (Matt. 25:14-30). Through this parable, Jesus teaches us that God gives each of us particular gifts to share with others. The parable tells of a man, who prior to leaving for a long journey, gives each of his slaves a number of talents, each talent worth many days' wages. The man gives his first slave five talents, the second two talents, and the third one talent. He instructs each slave to do with his talents what he can. The first two slaves invest their talents and increase their gifts. The third is scared and hides his one talent away, burying and wasting it. When the master returns, he expresses his pleasure with the first two slaves but his fury with the third because he has done nothing with his gift.

Read Matthew 25:14-30.

With which slave do you identify?

What gifts has God given you that you do or do not use?

As the master did with the slaves, God endows each of us with unique gifts, talents, and abilities. Our talents are precious and unique gifts entrusted to our care. God wants us to use these gifts—these expressions of our uniqueness—in our lives so that they can grow stronger and make a difference in life. Our talents find expression and multiply only when we use them in our own unique ways. All of us have the gift of love, which we express through our other gifts. Some of us have gifts in organizing, while others have musical, artistic, and dramatic gifts. Others have the ability to analyze, teach, or solve problems. The list goes on and on. God calls each of us to accept his or her unique gifts and to discover ways to express them throughout life. This acceptance and discovery require a willingness to affirm our uniqueness instead of denying it.

We deny our uniqueness in two ways: either by overemphasizing or by deemphasizing our worth as individuals. Glorifying our individual achievements in the pursuit of notoriety or acclaim denies our uniqueness by ignoring the fact that our gifts come from God, not from ourselves. We act as though we created our unique gifts and they exist only to serve our own aims and desires. In a capitalistic society that manufactures so many celebrities, it is easy to believe that money, fame, and power make us eternally more important than others.

God calls each of us to accept his or her unique gifts and to discover ways to express them throughout life.

We can also deny our uniqueness by allowing a group, community, or another person to control us and recreate us in their image. We let others deny our worth and uniqueness in many ways. For example, cults deny individuality and uniqueness by forcing members to comply with certain rules and principles. The denial of uniqueness and individuality has also been an inherent problem in communism, the Nazi movement, and all other communal attempts to deny the individual while emphasizing the whole. In addition, emotionally and physically abusive people crush their spouses' sense of unique worth by forcing them to ignore or devalue their gifts. The same is true of abusive supervisors in the workplace or companies that treat their workers as though they are worthless. Often people who overvalue their worth abuse those who undervalue their worth. They attract each other.

The expression of uniqueness in our daily activities influences how much our faith deepens and grows. Using our gifts, even in small and humble ways, strengthens our ability to connect with

God and follow God's path. Not using our gifts diminishes our ability to be God-sensitive and God-directed. We grow spiritually when we make choices that reflect our unique calling. We impede our spiritual growth whenever we ignore our unique calling by pursuing God substitutes.

What about personal attention do you find alluring?

In what areas have you found yourself seeking attention instead of your calling?

Take time to reflect and pray about this.

Many of us ignore our unique calling and our spiritual yearnings. We have become a culture that worships the individual—the celebrity, superstar, or millionaire—while ignoring our unique calling to be who God created us to be.

An interview with the basketball star Dennis Rodman reminded me of this. Rodman has become notorious for his outrageous antics. He dyes his hair different colors, sports many tattoos, and wears pierced earrings in a variety of body parts. The interviewer asked Rodman if there was anything that he really wanted to do in his basketball career. Rodman replied that someday he would like to take off all of his clothes and walk naked off the basketball court after a game. His comment was something to the effect of, "If I did that, then people would remember me. They would say to each other, 'That Dennis Rodman, he was an individual. He wasn't afraid to express himself.'" Being noticed was what mattered to Rodman. Rather than expressing gratitude for his God-given skills and abilities and for the opportunity to use them, Rodman focused on receiving attention. He gazed with praise upon himself, not God. Unfortunately too many of us worship at the altar of individualism. According to Adrian van Kaam, when the tradition of individualism controls us, it "deforms human life into an arrogant, isolating, sometimes bellicose enterprise. It separates us from one another, from the cosmos, and from [God]."[7]

Our overemphasis on individuality has produced a distrust of most institutions, which erodes the fabric of our culture and society.

The Nourishing Waters of Tradition

Our overemphasis on individuality has produced a distrust of most institutions, which erodes the fabric of our culture and society. Because so many people in our public institutions have sought their own agendas and been caught up in scandals and conspiracies, our culture distrusts government, business, religion, schools, the postal service, utility companies, the police, and many other institutions. This is not to say that we should revere these institutions, but we have moved to an opposite extreme in which we cynically condemn our public institutions no matter what they do.

In 1933 Eberhard Arnold, a German Hutterite (a Christian Anabaptist sect that emphasizes living in community), looked at the state of the world and declared, "The human race finds itself in such boundless misery because it has fallen into a state of hostility. It is split apart, lacerated. The cleft shows the disastrous degree to which coldness of heart and hostility [have] advanced in a divided humankind."[8] Arnold might look at today's culture and make the same declaration. We have allowed individualistic agendas to separate and divide people from one another, in many cases generating great hostility.

How are you tempted to deny your own uniqueness?

Do you tend to focus too much or too little on your own self-worth?

Individualism not only cuts us off from God; it cuts us off from the nurturing power of spiritual *traditions* that teach us how to live life in harmony and consonance with God. Adrian van Kaam has emphasized the crucial nature of traditions for our lives. He notes that plants have a genetic packaging that leads them to grow, produce, and reproduce. Animals have instincts and conditioning that cause them to behave in certain ways. In contrast, humans have relatively weak instincts and conditioning.[9] We compensate by developing our abilities to think and choose. Genetics and conditioning constrain animals and plants, which have almost no choices in life. But we always have some choice. While we depend upon our insight to make choices, traditions teach us how to form and develop our insights. We can loosely define traditions as the guiding sets of principles, customs, mores, norms, values, and laws that show us how to live our lives. Without traditions, we cannot make choices because we have nothing upon which to base our choices.

When we speak of traditions, we are not speaking simply about customary ways of doing things. For instance, while Aunt Mae's bringing her world-class cherry pie to the family reunion every year may be a family custom, a tradition refers to a larger body of philosophical and theological teachings that guides us and teaches us how to live. We all follow a set of *form* and *faith traditions* that guide us in our physical, psychological, spiritual, relational, and social development and formation.[10] Faith traditions are the overall beliefs we hand down from age to age: for instance, the belief that God created us, that Moses led the Israelites out of Egypt, and that Christ died for our sins. Form traditions are the particular traditions we hand down to our children regarding *how* we should pray, worship God, and express our faith. Faith and form traditions, whether religious or philosophical sets of beliefs, teach

What traditions heavily influence your life?

How deeply does the Christian faith tradition influence your life in comparison to other traditions such as democracy, capitalism, conservatism, liberalism?

us to live more harmoniously by incorporating particular ideals, values, and practices into our lives.

Faith and form traditions surround us. Capitalistic and democratic traditions deeply influence our lives in America. In addition, we find ourselves surrounded by religious faith traditions, ethnic traditions, as well as ideological and philosophical traditions.

As individuals, each of us follows certain traditions that we rank in terms of influence on our lives.[11] The most influential traditions provide a foundation that affects the extent to which we follow other traditions. For example, as a Christian, I try to place the Christian faith tradition at my foundation. Of less influence, but certainly of great influence, is the Presbyterian expression of this faith tradition. As a person trained in counseling and therapy, I also incorporate certain psychological and counseling traditions into my life. At one time, before I returned to the church, these psychological traditions were stronger and more influential in my life than the Christian traditions. Psychology was my religion. When I joined a church at age twenty-four, I had a hard time letting Christian beliefs become the foundation for my life.

Try drawing a pyramid with the most influential traditions in your life at the base, the least influential at the tip, and the others in between with the more influential ones towards the bottom.

As a United States citizen, I find that democratic and capitalistic traditions also lie very near my foundation. Of less influence (but certainly important nonetheless) are certain social, ethnic, and familial traditions. My rearing in the northeast United States allows me more comfort with a faster pace of life. As a person of largely Scottish heritage, traditions emphasizing stubbornness, stoicism, and skepticism have influenced me. As a person from a relatively boisterous family, I am fairly comfortable with arguments and heated discussion. Therefore, many traditions affect the choices I make. While I maintain some freedom to choose, each of these traditions teaches me how to live my life.

Confusion may result from internal clashes that take place between the various traditions we follow. Some of our Christian ideals clash with some of our capitalistic ideals, and some of our democratic ideals may clash with some of our business and organizational ideals. How do we decide which traditions should influence our lives the most? Clashes between traditions may encourage us to avoid making commitments to traditions, groups, practices, and directions even though they influence our lives positively. The absence of a strong faith or form tradition can lead us to follow individualism by default. Thus, as Wade Clark Roof has pointed out, we become wary and cautious about making commitments to any institutions.[12] We also avoid making commitments even to those traditions that deepen our faith, our spiritual lives, and our relationship with God.

The difficulty of making a full commitment to a guiding faith tradition is not a new phenomenon. The story of Jonah explores this issue in depth. While steeped in the Jewish faith tradition that taught him to obey and follow God, Jonah has developed a tremendous hatred of the Assyrians. The Jews and the Assyrians have been enemies for years, with strong nationalistic traditions of mutual loathing in both societies. Jonah has always been a faithful prophet. One day God says to Jonah, "Go at once to Nineveh, that great city, and cry out against it; for their wickedness has come before me" (Jon. 1:2). Jonah knows that God will spare Nineveh if its people repent. He is torn between his allegiance to God and his allegiance to the Hebrew tradition of hating the Assyrians. What should he do? Should he follow God and save his enemies, or rebel against God and kill his enemies? He decides to follow his hatred and runs from God in the hope that God will destroy the Ninevites.

Can you think of a time when you adhered to a destructive tradition that caused you to rebel against God?

Take time to talk with God about it.

God does not let Jonah go that easily. God pursues Jonah and causes a great fish to swallow him. Jonah relents and goes to Nineveh and cries out, "Forty days more, and Nineveh shall be overthrown!" (Jon. 3:4). The people of Nineveh listen and, proclaiming a great fast, change their ways. As a result, God spares them. Jonah's hate, nurtured by Israel's nationalistic traditions, erupts in fury. He goes off and sulks beneath a tree in anger, furious at God. Jonah's problem is that his commitment to Israel's nationalistic traditions is stronger than his commitment to his Jewish religious tradition and to God. He has lost his ability to discern the truly worthwhile commitment.

What kinds of commitments have you made in your life?

How have they helped you grow spiritually?

Making Commitments

To deepen our faith, we have to distinguish between the commitments that can nurture and guide us and those that will distract us. One thing is certain: We cannot move along our journey of faith without a willingness to make commitments. We have to commit to a relationship with God and to the things that foster that relationship. We also have to commit ourselves to particular life directions and to practices that will nurture that commitment.

Commitments channel our freedom. Our lives reflect our commitments. Our commitments to spiritually, physically, and mentally healthy traditions, groups, relationships, and ways of living shape our lives in healthy ways. Spiritually healthy commitments allow us to be formed by particular people, groups, ideals, causes, or ideologies.[13] The questions we ask each other when meeting for the first time reveal the importance of commitments: "What do you do? Where do you work? Are you married? What do you do in your spare time?" Essentially we ask about commitments: "To what or to whom do you commit your life?"

In the spiritual journey, our religious commitments deepen our relationship with God. Are we involved in a church? Do we pray? Are we involved in charitable ventures? Our religious commitments matter. When we make religious and spiritual commitments, we let faith traditions and communities teach us how to forge a deeper sensitivity to the ways God acts in our lives.

For Christians, one of the most important commitments is commitment to a church. By participating in a church, we allow the traditions, rituals, relationships, and responsibilities of the church to deepen our faith. We honestly have to admit that churches are always imperfect communities. Some are weaker than others, but even the greatest churches have shortcomings. Churches are flawed because people are flawed.

I have a theory about churches: If we want perfect churches, we have to get rid of the people; yet once we get rid of the people, we no longer have churches. We have to remember that every church is more than its flaws. We need to focus on the beauty that can emerge from even the most flawed church.

The Blessed Community

Despite their imperfection, most churches are in touch with God at a deep level. The Quaker Thomas R. Kelly calls this deep spiritual level of the church the "blessed community."

Despite their imperfection, most churches are in touch with God at a deep level. The Quaker Thomas R. Kelly calls this deep spiritual level of the church the "blessed community."[14] The blessed community is the core of a church that is deeply connected to God. Those members who place loving God at the center of their lives—who live to serve God in prayer and action—comprise the core. These people often work behind the scenes, remaining unnoticed by most church members. Kelly notes that many of the people involved in a church may not be connected to this essential core. Many of the most active church leaders are not part of this blessed community. Being active in a church does not necessarily connect a person with the blessed community that keeps a church alive. The spiritual core of a church, by virtue of its love for God, spreads God's blessings upon everyone else in the church. Every church and spiritual community has at least a few members who live in this blessed community.

Can you sense a blessed community in your church?

How does it affect the life of your church?

One woman told me about the church of her youth and its blessed community. She grew up during the Great Depression and was a member of a small church that kept growing despite hard times. She believed that the people at the spiritual core of her church were responsible for its growth. Every Monday morning, four women came to the church to pray for the church, its members, and for all in need of God's help. Their faith opened the church to receive God's grace.

The people who form a church's blessed community love others in the church and reveal God through their actions. Sometimes this core is a great fire that burns brightly, and sometimes it is a hot ember that smolders at the center of what seems like ashes. Whatever its form, this core group of people helps others enter a communal relationship with God. The blessed community inhabits the center of a church, rejoicing in the unity of God's love and transcending the theological and doctrinal differences that typically divide and alienate Christians from one another.[15]

I know a church in which two women maintained a bitter feud for many years. Both were active members, but they could not be in the same room together without getting into an argument. They remained in the same church but avoided each other religiously. Each took every opportunity to criticize the other behind her back. Did either woman remember the original reason for their feud? Probably not, but their anger had gained a life of its own.

Read Galatians 6:1-10, which speaks about those who are immersed in the blessed community.

What does it say are the characteristics of those who embrace this blessed community?

One Sunday after a sermon on forgiveness and reconciliation, the time came for Communion. As the pastor recited the words of institution, one of the women stood up and walked to the back of the church. The other woman got up and also walked to the back of the church. There they confronted each other, and in a moment that can only have arisen out of the blessed community, they embraced each other and began to cry. God's love that lay at the core of the church from its founding suddenly welled up and flowed through their embrace and their tears.

There are no coincidences, only providences.

Even commitment to the most flawed church can help us grow spiritually. Would either of these women have achieved that kind of reconciliation and forgiveness if she had left the church and chosen to go her own way? The women's commitment to the community created the conditions for their eventual reconciliation.

What qualities of faith communities and churches allow them to nurture us on our faith journeys? Churches offer us opportunities for love and reconciliation that we might miss otherwise. When we isolate ourselves from these communities spiritually, we also insulate ourselves from their spiritually nurturing power. Churches prevent us from becoming spiritually individualistic and narcissistic by connecting us with others who help deepen our faith. We can become discouraged in our faith more easily when alone than with others. Those who take their faith seriously will encounter periods of confusion, pain, discouragement, fear, and trepidation. When we are alone in our spiritual journey, we may be tempted to focus on other matters while ignoring our faith. When we walk with others in a faith community, we find brothers and sisters who support and care about us even when we feel hopeless.

Places of Providence

What kind of providences have you experienced in your life?

How has your church helped you sense them and become more sensitive to them?

Churches provide places where we can steep ourselves in nourishing faith traditions and share in God's love, and they are places in which incredible providences occur. I once heard Adrian van Kaam—a person I consider to be a spiritual beacon—say in a conversation, "There are no coincidences, only providences." I had an experience shortly thereafter that demonstrated the truth of this statement. In a sermon, I told a true story about a young man who described himself as a nihilist—a person who believes in nothing. I had read this man's story in a book. I neither knew him personally, nor had I ever heard of him before. I talked about how this man's life had become purposeless and destructive because he had ignored not only the need for faith but had actively sought a life without faith in anything. While he was proud of his nihilistic stand, his life was anything but wonderful.

After the worship service, a visitor with tears in her eyes asked to speak with me. When we met, she told me that she had been involved with the man I had mentioned in my sermon. He had inflicted tremendous psychological and spiritual damage on her life. After the initial shock of hearing me talk about this man from her past, the woman began to reflect on her own life. She told me how much she needed God in her life, and how this man represented her life without God. She also reflected upon how deeply God had touched her during a difficult period of her life. This "coincidence" led her to join our church, a place of understanding and healing. This woman's testimony affirms that churches are places of providence. During my ministry I have been amazed at how often providential coincidences consistently occur.

Places of Worship and Exercise

In addition to being places of providence, church communities also deepen our faith by giving us opportunities to exercise and strengthen our faith. Many of us claim to love everyone; a church setting calls us to make good on that claim. We normally surround ourselves with people we enjoy who are much like ourselves. Becoming part of a church community requires that we try to love people we might otherwise ignore. Churches are fascinating places filled with an odd collection of people: introverted and extroverted, obsessive and apathetic, alcoholic and abstaining, angry and happy, calm and skittish, liberal and conservative. At every turn we face Christians unlike us. Part of our commitment to the community involves learning to care about people who make us uncomfortable. Churches become places to test our love and our faith—to test our love for God in our love for others.

How are you at really loving those who are different from you?

Do you just ignore them, or do you treat them with love and respect even if they irritate you and treat you with a lack of respect?

Luke's Gospel stresses the importance Jesus places on practicing our love in difficult places. Jesus says to his followers,

> "If you love those who love you, what credit is that to you? For even sinners love those who love them. If you do good to those who do good to you, what credit is that to you? For even sinners do the same. If you lend to those from whom you hope to receive, what credit is that to you? Even sinners lend to sinners, to receive as much again. But love your enemies, do good, and lend, expecting nothing in return" (Luke 6:32-35).

Committing ourselves to a church community forces us to learn to love and to do good for those we might otherwise ignore and avoid. We may decide to leave a church because we see too many Christian hypocrites. Staying in a church forces us to learn to love them, and we come to see them as struggling souls rather than as hypocrites. Real love emerges. When we meet those unlike ourselves in church, we learn to love.

Dietrich Bonhoeffer wrote about the love we forge in the church by distinguishing between spiritual and human love.[16] He said that *human love* is a self-centered love that loves another only for our own sake, for what we expect in return. Human love is a controlling love. When we act out of *spiritual love,* we care about another person for Christ's sake, because Christ calls us to love that person. As Bonhoeffer stated,

> Where Christ bids me to maintain fellowship for the sake of love, I will maintain it. Where his truth enjoins me to dissolve a fellowship for love's sake, there I will dissolve it, despite all the protests of my human love. Because spiritual love does not desire but rather serves, it loves an enemy as a brother.[17]

Church communities, however flawed, guide us and give us opportunities to act out spiritual love.

Places of Listening

Isolating ourselves from a church often isolates us from the rich source of spiritual conversation that reveals the Holy Spirit.

Finally, participation in a church community offers us wonderful opportunities to hear God's spirit speak through ourselves and others. Isolating ourselves from a church often isolates us from the rich source of spiritual conversation that reveals the Holy Spirit. Leaving a church to discover God on our own is like going out into a desert to seek food—there is just not much there. If a person wants to find food, it is best to go to places that produce food. Similarly, a person who wants to grow spiritually needs to surround himself or herself with those who can reveal the Spirit through their voices.

I believe that one of the most powerful ways the Holy Spirit speaks to us in life is through conversation. Sometimes the Spirit speaks through my words; more often the Spirit speaks through the words of others. When we place ourselves in community, we discover many people speaking words of the Spirit—not only in sermons but in committee meetings, support groups, conversations over coffee, and all other activities. Our refusal to become part of a church family makes it much more difficult for the Spirit to speak to us.

Church communities are crucial to our faith journeys because the community of faith shares our journeys. An excellent metaphor for this shared journey is that of a flock of geese flying overhead. On their journeys southward, geese fly in a "V" or wedge formation. The lead goose bears the greatest load, deflecting the wind to both sides, cutting the wind resistance and creating a tiny drag behind it that eases the strain on the other geese. The further back a goose is from the front, the easier the flight. After a while, a goose in the back relieves the former lead goose, which moves back into the wedge formation. Each goose in the flock takes a turn as leader and follower. In addition, the geese honk constantly as a way of encouraging the lead goose. All that honking we hear is the other geese shouting, "Go on! You can make it. Fly, fly, fly!" Like a flock of geese in flight, churches help us move along on our journey. Sometimes we lead, and sometimes we follow. Either way we discover people who encourage us.

Participation in a faith community offers us an opportunity to balance and temper our individuality.

Church communities provide places for us to commit ourselves to the journey of falling in love with God. Despite their flaws, they help us become more open to God, God's grace, and God's love.

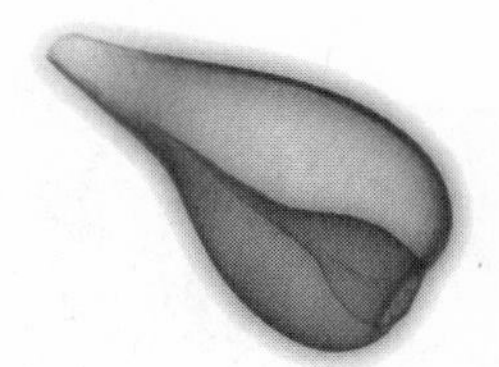

In our faith journeys, totally eradicating our individuality in favor of community can be detrimental to our spiritual health. But participation in a faith community offers us an opportunity to balance and temper our individuality. Church members can help us rediscover our uniqueness and more genuinely express God in and through our lives. Members of a spiritual community must respect our individuality and our uniqueness.

Commitment tempered by our openness to God is key. Rigid commitment can harm our spiritual growth as much as a lack of commitment can.Commitment to community can direct our lives and channel our energies in ways that deepen our faith by helping us become the unique persons God has created us to be.

Seven
Thankful Living

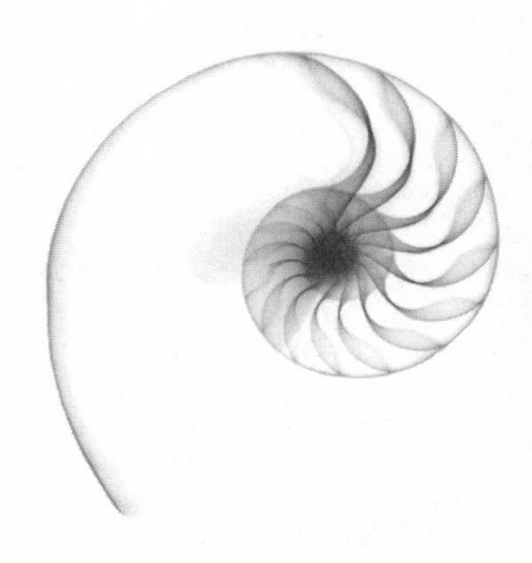

SEVERAL YEARS AGO I read about a remarkable woman who had received an award for her lifetime of devotion to others. She actively participated in her church, her local community, and throughout the area. What made the story so amazing was that this woman continued to receive such acclaim even while undergoing intensive treatments for cancer at a local hospital. In keeping with her nature, this woman did not let her disease stop her from caring for others. Instead, her struggles with cancer seemed to add to her ability to care for others. She seemed to draw strength from her illness.

Apparently this woman, so full of love and joy, used her own disease to deepen her compassion and to become more sensitive in her care for others. She inspired the nurses on her unit with her healing effect on other cancer patients. However, the nurses did have one problem with her: She was never in her room. She was too busy visiting and comforting other patients on the unit. They tried to take care of her, but the woman always shifted the focus from herself to the nurses, eventually caring for them more than they cared for her. She remembered every detail of their lives, asking about their children, girlfriends, boyfriends, or spouses. When the interviewer asked how she could focus on others while ignoring her own problems, the woman responded that it was easy. God had given her such a wonderful gift by giving her life that she wanted nothing more than to share and remind others of that gift.

The woman died of cancer several months after the article appeared in the newspaper. How could this woman be so loving when she was suffering herself? Didn't she know that she was dying? The cynics among us might suggest that she was just denying her own illness and mortality. Perhaps her care for others was a defense mechanism. Maybe she was compensating for her despair by putting on a cheerful face and adopting a cheerful attitude. Maybe she had a martyr complex. Perhaps this was all a front—a psychologically unhealthy avoidance of reality.

We can understand why some would jump to these conclusions. The woman did not act the way most of us would in similar circumstances. A man once told me that if he ever developed a grave illness and knew that he would certainly die, he would kill himself. Another person expressed concern about her ability to cope with terminal illness or incapacitation. She hoped that someone would "pull the plug" or "put her away." So what enabled this remarkable woman to respond to her illness in such a radically different way? What enabled her caring response to others? Was it just psychological denial and repression, or was it something more?

I believe it was something more. While I did not know this woman, I have had the privilege of knowing other remarkable people whose motivation during serious illness had a spiritual source. These people saw beyond the constraints that most of us place around our lives. They did not submit to the destructive and damaging power of disease. Instead they chose to give themselves over to the love of God. They chose to open themselves to God's grace, not death's despair. This reaction to crisis is uncommon today. While many people suffering from illness and disease try to maintain a positive outlook, the mood of our present culture often leads us in different directions.

How do you respond to difficulties?

Do troubles bury you, or do you find yourself looking toward God and God's grace?

Take time to reflect on this.

Looking through Cynical Eyes

We live in cynical times, full of confusion and uncertainty. The old answers to personal, relational, and social problems are no longer adequate. Often we respond to this confusion and uncertainty by withdrawing and taking care of ourselves, our immediate family, and our friends. During times of change and conflict, responding to problems by reaching out and caring for others is not easy. At one time our culture seemed more optimistic than it is now (maybe not more caring but certainly more optimistic). As a child I sensed such optimism in society. It seemed that no problem could arise that science, technology, and social action could not meet. We often heard phrases like, "Where there's a will there's a way," and "Nothing is impossible if you put your mind to it."

The phrases of our current culture reflect our inability to solve problems: "Every politician is a crook." "You can't trust anybody these days." "People just want something for nothing." "Nobody cares nothing about nobody no how!" People once optimistically looked for problems to solve, yet today—especially with many nontechnological problems—we worry that no solutions exist. New diseases pop up that seem to have no cure, and those that are curable are becoming resistant. Social problems, such as violence and drugs, seem to increase with each passing year. We have a tremendous distrust of politicians and politics. Conflict and terrorism face us at home and abroad, and we do not know how to respond. The gap between rich and poor seems to be growing. The advertising and entertainment industries bombard us with messages telling us that we are not thin enough, strong enough, sexy enough, smart enough, or wealthy enough; and these messages are wrapped in commercials and programs that embrace conflict and violence. The advertisers play on our insecurities by implying that something is wrong with who we are and what we have. Then we begin to feel angry and dissatisfied with our lives.

All of these seemingly unsolvable problems lead many of us to feel helpless, confused, and uncertain about our lives as we struggle to eke out a more perfect life. Our sense of helplessness and confusion has caused many of us to become cynical and even angry about our lives and our situations. The angry new mood in America has profoundly affected every aspect of our culture—including religious life. This pervasive anger can exert a debilitating power over our faith and our spirituality.

All of these seemingly unsolvable problems lead many of us to feel helpless, confused, and uncertain about our lives as we struggle to eke out a more perfect life.

From Cynicism to Appreciation

Whether we live in good times or bad, God does not call us to live in anger or cynicism. We receive assurances of this fact throughout the Bible. In Ecclesiastes we read, "Do not be quick to anger, / for anger lodges in the bosom of fools" (7:9). In Ephesians we read, "Do not let the sun go down on your anger, and do not make room for the devil" (4:26-27). Many of the biblical writers acknowledge anger as a natural human emotion. At the same time, they acknowledge that when it becomes unbalanced and disproportionate, anger is unhealthy. When anger and

Reflect on your own life.

Take time to get a sense of the degree of anger and frustration you have about your life and about life in general.

cynicism dominate us, they can damage and destroy our lives—especially our spiritual lives.

Many experts in the fields of psychology, relationships, and personal growth suggest that a more helpful and healthful response to change would be to adopt a more positive attitude for our lives. Psychological researchers notice that maintaining a positive attitude and a high level of self-esteem improves life. Most therapists are trained to monitor levels of self-esteem and self-confidence and to help clients develop a sense of hope.[1]

In her book *Pathfinders*, Gail Sheehy (a journalist with a background in human development) reports on the lives of people who have successfully navigated life's difficulties. As part of her research, she looked at the personal qualities that help people successfully overcome and move beyond the hardships, failures, and problems of life.[2] In all cases, these "pathfinders" exhibited a positive attitude and outlook towards life. Sheehy noted that they found a sense of meaning in their lives even during times of hardship. No matter how difficult life had become, they maintained a sense of purpose and direction. Sheehy discovered other positive qualities. These persons

People who overcome crises, transitions, and traumas seem to exhibit and exude an ability to see potential in any situation.

- approached transitions in creative and positive ways,
- were not dismayed by failure,
- tended to be pleased with their personal growth and development,
- felt a strong sense of love for family and friends,
- tended to be cheerful,
- expressed no major fears.

Thus, people who overcome crises, transitions, and traumas seem to exhibit and exude an ability to see potential in any situation. All of these characteristics certainly describe the hospitalized woman mentioned earlier. She did not let cancer hold her back. She responded to the crisis of her disease with a positive and meaningful outlook. Remaining upbeat and caring about others did not prevent her death, but it did bring a certain quality and hopefulness to her life.

People who successfully overcome difficult times also seem to have an ability to let go of cynicism, anger, and helpless feelings by adopting a sense of possibility and opportunity. They respond to moments and periods of crises in new, creative, positive, and transformed ways.

Many of us feel trapped in chronically detrimental patterns of living, but a friend of mine showed me that we all possess the ability to change our lives by changing our attitudes. As part of the research for her doctoral dissertation, Ellen explored an incident from her past in which she changed her chronic sense of anger into an attitude of possibility.[3] Several years ago Ellen went to a local post office in a poor and somewhat dangerous part of town to do some bulk mailing. She walked into the post office and immediately felt anxious as she examined her surroundings. Standing in the back of a line, she felt threatened by the starkness of the room and the angry-looking people around her.

When she got to the front of the line, a two-inch-thick bullet proof glass separated her from the postal clerk. Saying very little, she slid her mailings to the clerk through a slot in the glass. Speaking through the glass, the clerk told her the mailing cost. After accepting the money, the clerk slid the mailings back with a sheet of stamps. Pointing to a desk, she said, "You can put the stamps on over there." Already feeling tense and discouraged about much in her life, Ellen angrily shouted back, "Don't you do that?" Responding with equal anger, the clerk said, "No, you have to do your own stamps!"

How do you respond to difficulties in your life?

Are you able to maintain a positive outlook?

Take time to reflect on your attitude toward life.

At that point Ellen felt a conflict. Was this the way she should be treating another person? Should she let fear and anger control her actions? Her anger had gotten the better of her just as it had throughout much of her life. She thought for a moment and then said, "I'm sorry. I guess I'm just tired, and this glass and everything just makes me feel afraid." The clerk's anger melted as she looked at her and said with compassion, "I know. It's hard with all of these security measures. We have had too many robberies. I'll tell you what. I'll go ahead and put these stamps on."

In that moment, Ellen realized something about herself. She recognized that she was more than just her anger. She recognized that she did not have to respond to life with anger and fear. She could respond to life positively instead. She could let go of her anger instead of letting it dominate her life. This awareness greatly impacted her life, transforming her relationships and outlook.

Becoming more positive can help us live happier and more successful lives. A positive mental state can lead to better physical health. But on a spiritual level, is simply having a positive attitude enough? Is there something more for us on a spiritual level?

From the Positive to the Appreciative

Current literature that emphasizes the need for a healthy body/mind/spirit connection often only stresses the body/mind connection. Many of today's researchers treat spirituality as an extension of psychological awareness because they do not know how to study God or the impact of religion. They emphasize what they know—the mind and the body. In that process they deemphasize God and relegate spirituality to a psychological experience that offers a sense of meaning. Psychological spirituality emphasizes valuable meditative practices and interior experiences, but God-seeking spirituality must go further.

Psychological spirituality emphasizes valuable meditative practices and interior experiences, but God-seeking spirituality must go further.

Spirituality has to do with a realm that transcends human physiological and psychological experience. It has to do with our relationship with the divine, the transcendent, and the spiritual. Spirituality's concern is the realm of God. When we link spirituality solely with the mind and body, we lose much that connects us with the spiritual. Healthy spirituality integrates the dimensions of body, mind, and spirit, which are intimately interconnected. To be human means to be fully physical, psychological, and spiritual in nature. While a positive outlook is important on a psychological level, we need to broaden that outlook on a spiritual level to include an appreciative and thankful spirituality.

In his first letter to the Thessalonians, the Apostle Paul utters a spiritual triad that could serve as a guiding force for us as we attempt to deepen spiritually. Paul says to the Thessalonians, "Rejoice always, pray without ceasing, give thanks in all circumstances; for this is the will of God in Christ Jesus for you" (5:16-18). When we rejoice, we practice the art of positive thinking. We adopt an attitude in which we look for joy and good in all circumstances. Paul asks us to *pray without ceasing*—to include God in every area of life. And finally, he calls on us to adopt an *appreciative spirituality,* which Susan Muto and Adrian van Kaam call "appreciation."

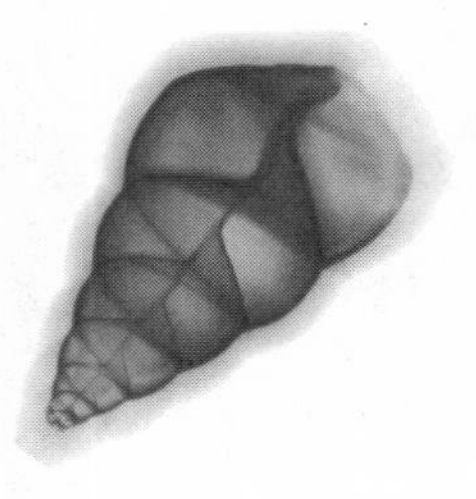

Appreciation is the art of seeking continually the "more than," while simultaneously moving away from the "less than."[4] When we become more appreciative, we begin to recognize value in life, the "more than" that transcends life or brings transcendent meaning to life. We pursue things, activities, perspectives, and beliefs that move us beyond the common constraints of life's struggles. We discover meaning in almost all circumstances. Appreciation of life, God, and ourselves helps us discover the meaning that can emerge from the death of a loved one, a beautiful sunset, the nourishing and awesome power of a thunderstorm, the visit of a friend, the opportunity to watch a sporting event, the satisfaction of doing a menial and unappreciated task well, or the frightening power of a hurricane.

An appreciative spirituality that pursues the "more than" teaches us to cherish God's spirit as it emerges in every facet of life.

An appreciative spirituality that pursues the "more than" teaches us to cherish God's spirit as it emerges in every facet of life. Our appreciation of God's continued grace and presence becomes unceasing prayer because it invites God into every aspect of life. Van Kaam and Muto suggest that the way to discover the "more than" lies in asking two important questions: "How do we make sense out of the events that shape our day-to-day existence? How can we develop an outlook that will help us to find lasting meaning in life?"[5]

Reflect on your life.

What kinds of things do you appreciate about your life?

What aspects of your life give you a sense of meaning?

Take time to thank God for them.

Pursuing the "less than," or the more depreciative aspects of life, means that we allow boredom, anger, resentfulness, jealousy, joylessness, apathy, complacency, and unchecked ambition to affect our lives adversely on physical, psychological, and spiritual levels. When we let these negative attitudes shape our lives, we do not live in the ways God calls us to live. We move away from the admonition to pray without ceasing. Being dominated by these emotions shuts off our prayer to God by pushing God out of our lives.

Unceasing Prayer

Continual prayer takes us beyond positive thinking by reconnecting us with God. Our cognizance of God in every area of life, invigorates our lives and sensitizes us to God's activity all around us. The story of an old French monastery demonstrates the power of unceasing prayer. For many years the monastery had been a vigorous and lively center for spirituality and faith. People came from all over Europe to learn from its monks. Over time, the monks became complacent and apathetic, and the monastery began to decline. As the decline worsened, the monks started to blame one another for their loss of centeredness. "If only the rest of you would adhere more faithfully to our disciplines," one monk said, "we would regain our former greatness." Another stated, "If only you would all pray more deeply, we would be in better shape." Still another said, "If only all of you

What are some of the negative emotions, situations, and practices that tend to make you depreciate your life and the world around you?

What causes you to feel joyless, apathetic, and resentful?

Take time to reflect on this.

would read your scriptures more often, we would be like we were."

They argued and argued, but nothing changed. Eventually only twelve monks remained in the monastery. One day, long after people had stopped visiting this former spiritual center, a stranger appeared at the monastery doors asking for shelter. That evening he ate with the monks and spent time with them in prayer. The next day he thanked the abbot, and as he was leaving he told the abbot something odd. "For your gracious hospitality, I want to tell you a secret. The Christ is one of you." The abbot was flabbergasted. What did this stranger mean? Was he deranged, or did he know something? Over the next few days the abbot told some of the other monks about this curious message from the stranger, and soon it spread like wildfire throughout the monastery.

Who could it be? the monks asked themselves. *Is it brother Joseph? No, he's much too lazy. Could it be brother Peter? No, he's too demanding*. They thought about each monk, and no one seemed to fit the model. Then they began to think, *Maybe Christ is just pretending to be lazy, demanding, stupid, or unfriendly*. Soon, in their fear of offending Christ, they began to treat one another as possible Christs. Over time a change in the monastery accompanied this change of perspective. As the monks began to treat one another with love and respect, the monastery began to attract visitors again. Soon people showed up asking to become monks, and within several years the monastery was once again a major center of spirituality.

How well do you sense Christ in others?

Think about the people who bother you the most. Can you sense Christ in them?

Read Matthew 3:21-26, 38-48.

What do these verses suggest about seeing Christ in others?

If the faith journey and the spiritual life are about falling more deeply in love with God, then beginning to sense God's presence in everything becomes crucial. Because the monks sensed Christ in one another, they actually began practicing Paul's call to pray unceasingly—to speak to, listen for, and spend time with God. This led them to appreciate one another more. Unceasing prayer does not mean necessarily saying a prayer over and over (although it can mean that). It means we make our whole lives a prayer, bringing God into every aspect of life. As the Anglican mystic Evelyn Underhill states, "A real man or woman of prayer, then, should be a live wire, a link between God's grace and the world that needs it.... One human spirit can, by its prayer and love, touch and change another human spirit; it can take a soul and lift it into the atmosphere of God."[6]

Vital Sensitivity to God

As we make our lives a prayer, we discover God revealed through three kinds of sensitivity. The first way that we become more sensitive to God is by appreciating the gift of life itself—by forming a *vital sensitivity*. We sense God in life through awareness of God in the creative vitality of life—in the "aliveness" of life. Through a vital sensitivity we increasingly recognize God as the creator and source of all life, and we develop awareness of the expressions of God's love throughout creation. We begin to perceive and appreciate the basic, God-given gift of life. We are more than just matter. God has made us alive, and we recognize that God expresses something of God's self through our specific gift. Furthermore, we begin to affirm every other person as a unique gift and expression of God's presence.

God's creative power is everywhere, and appreciating God in all of life deepens our sensitivity to God.

Appreciating God's presence goes beyond appreciation of human life to the recognition of the value of everything that is alive. God's creative power is everywhere, and appreciating God in all of life deepens our sensitivity to God. Therefore, we can become sensitive to God in the life of a dog, a kitten, a blue jay, an ant, a fish, a blade of grass, an oak tree leaf, a flock of geese, a cornfield, a forest, and a lake. Each is an expression of God and God's love, for God's creative power is the source of their being.

How vitally sensitive are you?

As you look around, do you recognize God's presence in yourself, in others, in nature, and in the universe?

Take time to pray about this and to ask God to increase your sensitivity.

During my family visits to a lake in Ontario every summer, I have become aware of God. I enjoy sitting by the lake late at night and gazing at the stars, which fascinate me because of their clarity. There are few nearby towns or cities to obscure the stars with lights, so the stars shine incredibly clear and brilliant in that northern air. Just to sit on the dock and contemplate these amazing stars helps me become deeply aware of how small I am and of how great God is—especially since God is greater than the stars and goes beyond the limits of our universe. To think that each star is as big as or bigger than our own sun, and to see how countless they are makes me conscious of how we limit God. Sometimes shooting stars and the northern lights punctuate this celestial show and add to my awe.

The stars are not alive in the sense that we normally think of life, yet they *are* alive in God's power. Because stars inhabit galaxies, the dynamic and immense power of gravity that maintains their swirling dance connects them. By virtue of their being in creation they are never static.

Exposing ourselves to nature nourishes our spiritual lives. Keeping ourselves rooted in life by surrounding ourselves with children or small pets, working in a backyard garden, enjoying walks through a park, taking drives through the country, allowing time to watch the birds at the feeder nourishes us spiritually. However we do it, exposing ourselves to life and nature helps us appreciate God's creative beauty all around us.

What experiences sensitize you to God?

Can you increase these experiences by taking more time to engage in them?

Take time to reflect on this possibility.

Symbolic Sensitivity to God

Vital sensitivity makes us more aware of God's creative power, and observing nature and life can lead to immediate experiences of God. Another way of becoming more sensitive to God lies in our receptivity to symbols in our lives—in becoming *symbolically sensitive.* While usually unaware of it, we are deeply symbolic creatures. Our need for symbols distinguishes us from animals that really do not see much in life beyond what their experience and instinct tell them. Humans, on the other hand, live and breathe symbols that tell us about the world and the universe around us. If a dog looks at the sky, it does not notice the stars. When I look at the stars, I see more than points of light. I see God, my own smallness and insignificance, the possibility of life on other planets, the beauty of the universe, and my own love of nature. The stars become more than just stars. They point to deeper meaning, express God's creative power, and become symbols of the "more than."

To appreciate our symbolic nature, we have to begin with language. We communicate in deeply symbolic ways. Look at this sentence. It is a collection of symbols. Each letter is more than a squiggle, a circle, or a line. It symbolizes a particular sound. As the letters merge to form words, the words themselves symbolize something more than a collection of letters. For example, when we write the word *cow*, we understand that this word refers to a grazing animal that provides us with food, milk, and leather. Similarly, each word in a sentence, as it connects with other words, symbolizes ideas and concepts beyond the juxtaposition of words. Letters, words, and sentences are complex verbal symbols.

We also use nonverbal symbols. The shrug of a shoulder symbolizes confusion. A smile symbolizes happiness or pleasure. A touch of our hand on someone's shoulder can symbolize love.

Philosopher Paul Ricoeur has studied the power of symbols in human life. He says symbols help us grasp certain ideas and thoughts, especially abstract ones, and in so doing take us from one level of understanding to another.[7] When we see an object before us, we notice not only the object; we also recognize its symbolic significance. The shirt a woman wears is not only a piece of cloth that covers her body, but it symbolically tells me about that woman. Wrinkles, soil, and tears may tell me about her distress or economic status. Silk and fine fabrics may convey a sense of worldly importance. Symbols surround us, inform us, and form us.

How sensitive are you to God's symbolic voice?

What symbols of God do you see all around you?

What do they communicate to you?

Anything that becomes a symbol also expresses something about the world and the universe.[8] A shirt not only tells us something about the woman, but its colors symbolically tell us about the properties of light; its texture tells us about matter; and the fact that a person wears it tells us about the human need for clothing as a means of warmth, self-expression, and social acceptability. Each symbol expresses countless messages about life, the universe, and especially God. The more we attempt to understand things on the global, universal, and divine levels, the more we depend upon symbols. This makes symbols especially important in our relationship with God. Symbols give us a glimpse of a God who otherwise lies beyond our grasp. God recognizes this fact and communicates through symbols. Symbols help us understand what God has done and what God is doing.

Symbols give us a glimpse of a God who otherwise lies beyond our grasp. . . . Symbols help us understand what God has done and what God is doing.

Once, while worshiping in a Roman Catholic church, I began to study the crucifix behind the altar. Being Protestant, I do not often see crucifixes in church. Somehow the crucifix drew me. I studied it, especially the anguish on Jesus' face, the wound in his side. How frail and thin he seemed. I began to think about how we, like those who crucified Jesus, try to prevent God from being a creative and healing force in our lives. I began to wonder why God would care so much about us when we seem to care so little about God.

As I continued to meditate on the crucifix, I thought about the difference between a Roman Catholic crucifix and a Protestant cross. The Protestant cross symbolizes the empty cross of the Resurrection. God cares about us because God loves us. God knows that we will not reject God forever, just as God knew that the pain of crucifixion eventually gives way to the joy of resurrection. God knows that there is more to our relationship with God than pain, suffering, and rejection. God has an eternal hope that

each of us will stop rejecting God and eventually learn to love God with all our minds, hearts, souls, and strength. These insights came about because of the symbolic nature of the crucifix. God used the symbol of the crucifix to tell me something more directly, to communicate with me both from my environment and from within my heart.

Christians resonate with certain symbols readily, and we commune with God more or less continually through these symbols. The cross, the crucifix, the baptismal font, the scriptures, the pulpit, the communion table or altar, and various other Christian symbols tell us something about God, life, and ourselves. When we recognize these symbols, we develop a sensitivity to God, but symbols can lead us deeper.

We form a heightened sensitivity to God when we realize that anything in life can be a symbol for God. Through our symbolical sensitivity, we learn to sense God in everything around us at a deeper level. The more symbolically sensitive we become, the more God actively uses symbols to speak to us.

What everyday symbols does God reveal to you?

Reflect on your life and discover any particular sights, sounds, or smells that help you appreciate God more.

A digital clock reminds me of how God uses everyday symbols to speak to us. I learned to sense God symbolically through numbers while struggling through a difficult period of my life. One afternoon I was exercising on a cross-country ski machine. As I moved my arms and legs back and forth, I thought about how much I was struggling. I thought about all the difficulties in my life and wondered why God was not more active in removing them. I said to God, "Why are you making my life so hard? Can't you do something?" At that moment, I looked down at the mileage gauge, and it registered 3.33 kilometers. There was something wonderful about that number. The number three symbolizes the trinity, and these three 3s seemed to remind me of God's presence with me. In my heart, I felt comforted immediately, as though God were saying to me, "Don't worry. I'm with you no matter what happens." It may seem silly; but ever since, I have sensed God's presence every time I look at a clock that says either 3:33 or 33 minutes past the hour.

I could easily suggest that my mind is trying to manufacture meaning, but I know in my heart that God uses the clock to remind me of God's presence. What really amazes me now about this particular 333 symbol is how often I look at digital clocks at exactly 33 minutes past the hour—especially at 3:33 in the afternoon, or at 3:33 in the morning when I wake up and look at the clock. I don't look for it intentionally, but I find my attention drawn to clocks at these particular moments.

Becoming more sensitive to God's presence in symbols has taught me to look for God's activity throughout life. I see God in paintings, books, the number 33, music, films, my wife's laughter, a cross or crucifix, a church, the friendliness of a store clerk, and anything else that symbolizes God's voice and presence. Our symbolical sensitivity to God enables us to appreciate God's continued communication and action with us. God depends upon our symbolic sensitivity. When we cannot sense God, we are symbolically numb—at least to the divine and the spiritual. God uses symbols to break into the secular realm to draw us into the divine realm. Becoming symbolically sensitive opens us to God and God's word to us.

Epiphanic Sensitivity to God

A third way we can become more sensitive to God, and thus increase our appreciation of God in life, is by forming an *epiphanic sensitivity*. This is a sensitivity to how God is revealed directly throughout life. An *epiphany* is a manifestation or revelation of God—God's direct presence embodied in life. Jesus, as an epiphany, revealed God's embodied light. Christ still has the power to be embodied in our hearts and to reveal God and God's word. God enters our lives epiphanically by acting directly in the events of our lives, touching our lives through specific acts of inspiration, healing, and providence. Often we lack the receptivity to recognize this divine activity.

God enters our lives epiphanically by acting directly in the events of our lives, touching our lives through specific acts of inspiration, healing, and providence. Often we lack the receptivity to recognize this divine activity.

God inspires us by providing direct insights and directives, yet we often ignore them. Horace Bushnell, a nineteenth-century Congregationalist pastor, wrote about human inspiration and the inspirations of God's spirit. He recognized that all humans have a natural capacity for inspiration that allows an infusion of the higher nature of God.[9] These inspirations transform us as God responds to our immediate situations.[10]

When we ignore God and God's direct presence, we deny our capacity for inspiration and thereby block direct and nonsymbolic inspirations from the Holy Spirit. I have come to appreciate this sad reality as I have reflected upon my entry into seminary. Initially I had no interest in ministry whatsoever; I wanted to be a psychotherapist. As far as I was concerned, religion was for

Have you ever been inspired to do something unexpected in your life that made things better?

What happened?

Why did you listen?

Take time to reflect on this.

losers. However, at age twenty-four, I found myself completely disillusioned and burned out by my work as a therapist in a psychiatric hospital. All my life I had wanted to be a counselor. I had a job in my chosen profession, and I hated it. At one point I talked with my father on the telephone and complained about my inner turmoil. He responded by saying to me, "Graham, I had dinner recently with the president of a local seminary, and he told me about a program in which you can get a Master of Divinity [a ministry degree] and a Master of Social Work [a counseling degree] at the same time." I laughed at my father and said, "Dad, could you ever see me as a minister?" He responded, "Actually, yes." So I said, "Hah! There's no way it will ever happen."

Despite my rejecting this possibility, something about my father's suggestion tugged at me. Nine months later, I was still in turmoil and returned to this possibility. By this time, my interior struggles had led me to join a local church. With a much greater sense of humility and openness, I finally listened to the voice inside and decided to attend seminary. I initially had rejected the inspirations emerging from my heart that my father's words evoked. I had become epiphanically numb. But over time my inner turmoil led me to become more epiphanically sensitive, allowing me to follow God's guidance.

God acts directly in our lives not only by inspiring us but by healing us and by intervening providentially in life for us. We can never predict these healings and interventions. In acts of healing, for instance, God sometimes heals completely on a physical level, while at other times the healing comes in a spiritual fashion. God's healing actions are mysterious and seem to depend upon our epiphanic sensitivity.

God acts directly in our lives not only by inspiring us but by healing us and by intervening providentially in life for us.

A woman I know suffered for years from chronic fatigue syndrome, which left her feeling overwhelmed by constant fatigue and lack of energy. She had tried all cures and had contemplated suicide when she decided to visit a holy site in Europe. Reportedly many healings had occurred on this site. She went not knowing what to expect but with the hope that something would happen. With a "hesitant openness" that became a growing epiphanic sensitivity, she visited a local priest who prayed over her. Something wonderful happened. She felt a healing power like electricity go through her whole body, yet it did not prompt a physical healing. Instead, she heard God deep inside saying, "Everything will be all right. Just trust in me."

The woman experienced spiritual healing, and it came as an epiphany. Her fatigue stayed with her, but somehow she knew that this illness would no longer rule her life. She would overcome it. Now, years later, she has resumed an active life and has found life enjoyable and worth living again. While the healing was God's responsibility, her openness to God's healing touch allowed God to break through into the events of her life. Our epiphanic sensitivity helps us discover that God touches us with the gift of life and speaks to us through the events of life.

Are you willing to allow God to directly influence your life?

Reflect on this for a bit, and pray about it.

Vital, symbolic, and epiphanic sensitivity overlap. We must be sensitive to all the ways God acts in our lives. Vital sensitivity connects with epiphanic sensitivity, for God can be revealed through life and nature. Epiphanic sensitivity is symbolic because symbols directly reveal God. As we nurture one kind of sensitivity, we also nurture other kinds. Vital sensitivity increases our symbolic sensitivity; symbolic sensitivity strengthens our epiphanic sensitivity; and epiphanic sensitivity enables us to become more vitally sensitive.

Have you ever had a healing experience? Not necessarily a physical one, but one that suddenly made your life better—one that made you realize God was a healing presence?

What happened?

How open were you to God during that time?

Take time to reflect on this.

Becoming Thankful

Becoming more sensitive to God in all forms helps us adopt an approach to God that is crucial to our spiritual growth. It is not enough just to be more aware and sensitive to how God touches our lives. It is also important that we become thankful for what God has done. This touches on Paul's third instruction to us in his letter to the Thessalonians. He tells us to rejoice always, to pray without ceasing, and to *give thanks in all circumstances.* Many of us find giving thanks to be especially difficult when life is not going "our" way. Too often we withhold our thanks until God does what we want. In the process, we shut ourselves off from God. By practicing the discipline of thanking God continually, we not only become more sensitive to God's grace, but we receive it and accept it into our lives with a real sense of openness.

Living thankfully means living with a deep sense of receptivity to God. Paul Tillich talks about the power of receptive thankfulness and thanksgiving, noting that when we thank God for something, we make it holy: "Thanksgiving is consecration; it transfers something that belongs to the secular world into the sphere of the holy."[11] In gratitude we transfer our lives from the secular world to the sphere of the holy. Thankful living makes our lives more holy by opening every facet of our lives to God's continual grace, and we accept with joy all the ways God is working in our lives.

Gratitude is a primary way to become open to grace. The term *grateful* literally means "full of grace." Fifteenth-century spiritual writer Thomas à Kempis says, "Grace will always be given to the truly grateful."[12]

God waits around every corner of life with a surprise.

Giving thanks in all circumstances is truly a discipline; it is far easier to complain, moan, and grumble. We can complain that our career is not the way we want it to be; that our marriage is not as happy as we'd like; that we are growing old and our bodies do not work the way they used to; or that society does not have the stability we desire. When we focus on these problems, we miss the ways in which God acts to transform life. We also miss the many times God acts specifically in our own lives.

David Steindl-Rast, a Benedictine monk, suggests that we need to approach life not only with a sense of gratefulness, but with a sense of openness to surprise.[13] God waits around every corner of life with a surprise. We have to look for these surprises and be willing to accept them as gifts from God. We can allow life's problems and turmoils to consume us and ignore God's surprises. By simply looking up and around, we discover the many surprises that God gives us at each moment of life. Surprise and gratitude go together. Accepting God's surprises with gratefulness and thanks intimately connects us to God.

Take time to think about what you have to be thankful for in your life.

Afterward, pray and thank God for all that you have received.

When we thank God in all circumstances, we offer God our own gift. As Paul Tillich points out, a gift only becomes a full gift when it leads to a sense of mutual connection. By receiving a gift and offering thanks, we give something of ourselves back to the giver.[14] A bond between the two of us arises. The receiver of a gift is bound by acceptance of it, while the giver of the gift is bound by the other's gratitude. In effect, the giver and receiver of the original gift become bound as they receive and accept each other. Ultimately then, thankful living leads to a deeper sense of love between God and ourselves, bringing us back to the original part of Paul's triad to the Thessalonians—*rejoice always.* Through thankful living we rejoice throughout life because we know the deep love of God in our lives.

Eight

A Compassionate Faith

WHEN I WAS growing up during the 1960s and early 1970s, one prominent theme of the day was the idea that if we could just love one another, all our problems would disappear. Films, television, and music taught us that love would solve all of our problems. The Beatles sang, "All you need is love." James Taylor told us to "shower the people you love with love." Stevie Wonder assured us that "all in love is fair." Young people hoped that love would become a dominant force in the world and in their lives. Ironically, while popular culture extolled the virtues of love, acts of violence dominated the news. We witnessed assassinations, left-wing bombings, right-wing coups, foreign battles, urban unrest, and rising crime rates. How could our obsession with love have produced the violent society we live in today? Why was our focus on love such a failure?

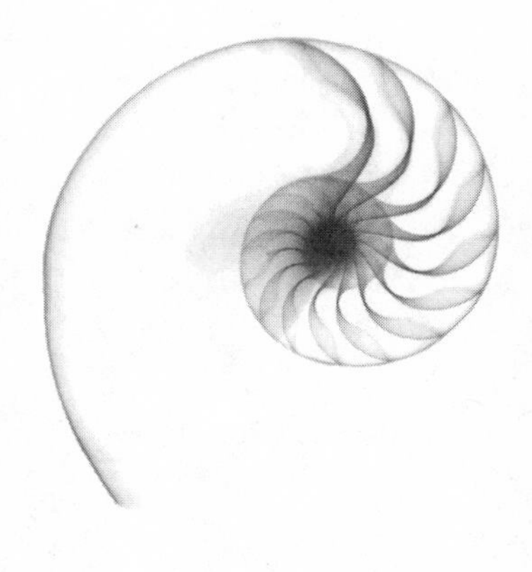

Part of the answer lies in the fact that not everyone who preached love was really talking about love at its deepest level. Some people's concern with love revolved around physical expression, and they chose to ignore the psychological and spiritual aspects of love. They confused physical contact with real love. Some people confused infatuation with love. They thought that the romantic feelings we experience at the beginning of a relationship were the same as those formed within a deep love of many years. Others confused thinking and talking about love with real love. They forgot that love is also a verb that requires action in life. These people often talked about loving others, but they had a hard time translating their thoughts and statements into concrete action. Still others convinced themselves that they loved others, but in reality they only loved people who resembled them. The shared love existed as long as others adopted similar appearances, practices, and interests.

How could our obsession with love have produced the violent society we live in today? Why was our focus on love such a failure?

We do not talk about love as much today, perhaps because we have learned from the sixties and seventies how difficult loving others can be. Today people tend to speak about love mainly in reference to close friends and family. We probably can address our divisions and differences better than we can talk about what we share. As Christians, we know that love is our bread and butter. Love is something we are supposed to exhibit not only toward others, but especially toward those who are our enemies. Simply put, we are called upon to love others no matter who they are. So as Christians, we face some difficult questions: If love is so important, why do we find it difficult to love others? What makes caring for and about people other than close friends and families so hard to do? In fact, why can't we love even close friends and family?

Reflect honestly on your own life.

Is loving others easy or difficult for you?

Who are some of the people you have a difficult time loving?

How well do you show your love to those for whom you care?

How do you treat those you do not love?

For the answers, we return to Luke's Gospel. In discussing faith, we looked at the passage in which a young lawyer asks Jesus how a person can gain eternal life. Jesus responds, "You shall love the Lord your God with all your heart, and with all your soul, and with all your strength, and with all your mind; and your neighbor as yourself" (Luke 10:27). We often read this passage from a functional or nonspiritual perspective. We hear a great charge telling us to love others as ourselves, a great moral challenge urging us to rise above our human constraints by loving others and treating them the same way we would like to be treated—not a bad interpretation but not the full message.

When all we hear is the need to love others as ourselves, then we approach love in a *willful* way. We see love as something we have to do by ourselves—something that takes willpower. For this reason, many of us simply give up on our attempts to love others. We learn from our failures that real love is impossible. Therefore, we say that loving others is an idealistic pipe dream; and in our attempts to be pragmatic, we care only about those who seem deserving. We see our love as too precious to waste on undeserving people. The more idealistic ones of us convince ourselves that we really do love all people. While we may believe that we love others, we cannot see how limited our love for others really is.

For most of us, our love fails because it is not rooted in the source of love—God.

Rooting Our Love in God

For most of us, our love fails because it is not rooted in the source of love—God. In our attempts to love others, we forget that it is God who gives birth to love, who nurtures love, and indeed who is love. We forget that Jesus tells us *first* to love God, and only then to love others as ourselves. The author of First John says,

> Whoever says, "I am in the light," while hating a brother or sister, is still in the darkness. Whoever loves a brother or sister lives in the light, and in such a person there is no cause for stumbling. But whoever hates another believer is in the darkness, walks in the darkness, and does not know the way to go, because the darkness has brought on blindness. (2:9-11)

How deep is your love for God?

This is never an easy question to answer, but it is crucial to deepening faith.

Take time to reflect on this and on ways that you can deepen your love for God.

These words remind us that just as God is light, expressions of God in life are always rooted "in the light." Actions devoid of God are rooted in human darkness. Hate, contempt, and disdain find their roots in darkness, not light. To become a deep part of human life, love must be rooted in the Light. It must be rooted in God.

A balanced faith journey always begins with a love of God that allows love to flow from God into us and through us to others. Whenever our love loses this flow, it begins to dry up. Rooting our love in a love of God keeps us connected to the source of love. Our love for others, instead of being willful and emerging only from our own efforts, grows out of our love for God. Love flows *through* us instead of originating *in* us.

A balanced faith journey always begins with a love of God that allows love to flow from God into us and through us to others.

When we recognize God as the source of love, we can become more accepting of the love of God that flows through others and into us. Many people will care for others but refuse care for themselves. By acknowledging that God loves us through others, we affirm God's direct love for us, as well as God's indirect love for us through the loving acts of friends, family, and strangers. A diagram for this flow of love follows:

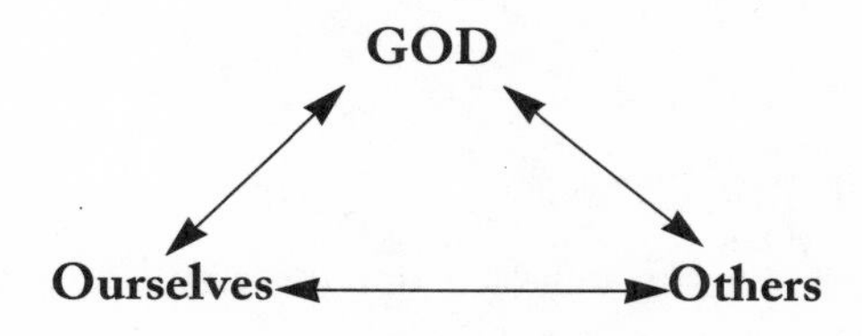

Crucifying God's Love

When love is really active in our lives, it flows among all three poles: God, ourselves, and others. Our love for God allows God's love to flow into us, and from us it can flow out to others. When other people have a strong love for God, love flows through them and into us. Sometimes we choose to crucify God's love by blocking God's ability to love us directly, to love us through others, and to love others through us. We can block love by ignoring God and God's gift of grace in our lives, by pushing God away, or by becoming overly self-critical. In these ways, we diminish God's love in our lives.

I have seen love and grace blocked during times of crushing grief, terrible suffering, and debilitating trauma. Heartbroken and distraught, we become angry at God for allowing this awful thing to happen, and we block God out of our lives. We perceive our misfortune as the unfair act of an uncaring God, thereby rejecting God and the comfort of God's healing love.

When have you crucified God's love?

Do you have difficulty recognizing how much God loves you?

Do you have trouble accepting the love of others?

Do you have a hard time showing others your love?

Take time to pray to God about how God's love could flow more freely through your life.

We not only block God's ability to love us when we reject God, but we block God's ability to love us through others when we cut others off. When we look upon others with contempt or derision, we block God's ability to love others through us. Anytime we block God's love from becoming a presence in the world, we crucify God's love. A diagram of crucified love looks like this:

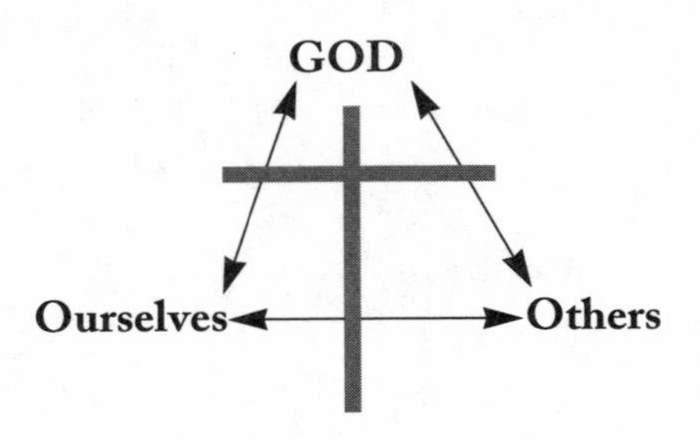

Spirituality and Caring

The strong connection between openness and love makes maintaining a balance between depth of spirit and active caring so important. In seeking spiritual growth, we easily can become spiritually self-focused. Too many of us who seek spiritual deepening only seek interior experiences. We want to learn how to pray, meditate, obtain spiritual gifts, and be inspired by God's spirit; but we do not necessarily expect these disciplines to change our exterior lives. An exclusive focus on interior spirituality may block the exterior expressions of love that a deep faith evokes.

Several years ago I turned on an afternoon talk show to hear a well-known actress discuss her disappearance from television and her subsequent spiritual wandering. In her depression over the cancellation of her television series and her inability to find work as an actress, she decided to take a trip to South America. There she met a guru who taught her to pray and meditate. She boasted that she could now meditate up to ten hours a day. She also remarked that her ability to pray had enabled her to overcome all sorts of psychological problems and difficulties.

Stories about people who rise above the tumult of their lives are heartening, but I was genuinely amazed that anybody could or would meditate for so long. I kept hearing the words of Mother Teresa that I read a long time ago in an interview. In answering a question about prayer, Mother Teresa suggested that if we spend three hours a day meditating, we need to reduce it by about two-and-a half hours so we can go out and care for others. Prayer's vital importance rests in its rooting us and connecting us with God. It is this connection, this relationship with God, that leads us to care for others. We cannot just hold God's grace inside. All of the personal spiritual insight in the world is wasted if it remains only an interior experience.

The writer of James asks us to connect our faith to our deeds:

> What good is it, my brothers and sisters, if you say you have faith but do not have works? Can faith save you? If a brother or sister is naked and lacks daily food, and one of you says to them, "Go in peace; keep warm and eat your fill," and yet you do not supply their bodily needs, what is the good of that? So faith by itself, if it has no works, is dead (2:14-17).

Doing good deeds will not save us, nor will God look on us with more love because we do good things. As this passage points out, the true good we do is a response to God, a response that arises from our faith. Faith leads a person to act in concrete, loving ways. Love of God leads to a love of others. If our love of God does not lead us to love others more, then we need to deepen our love for God. Faith begins with God and flows outward in acts of compassion. God's compassion for us inspires our compassion for others.

Faith begins with God and flows outward in acts of compassion. God's compassion for us inspires our compassion for others.

I and Thou

The roots of compassion, then, are planted in our relationship with God. Our compassion grows as our love for God grows, and our compassion shrinks whenever we insulate ourselves from God. One writer who truly understood the power both of connection and separation was the Jewish philosopher Martin Buber. In his original and insightful book *I and Thou,* Buber described how we naturally seek a relationship with the divine and with others, yet we also tend to insulate ourselves from the divine and from others. In Buber's terms, humans usually approach each relationship either from an *I-Thou* or an *I-It* perspective. These two perspectives oppose each other and lead to vastly different kinds of relationships.[1]

In the *I-It* relationship we regard people and things as less important than we are. We treat them as objects. Regarding an object as an *it* is appropriate when dealing with actual things. For instance, we should treat a car as an object that serves us. A car is not alive, nor is it human (despite the fact that some people name their cars and may treat them better than the people in their lives). By its very nature, we treat a car as an *it.*

While we appropriately treat things as objects—as *its*—it is inappropriate to treat fellow human beings in this way. We should not treat people as objects. We also could refer to Buber's *I-It* relationships as *I-He* or *I-She* relationships. In these relationships, the other person is disconnected from us. Buber attempts to show that when we regard people in this way, we treat them as objects. We do not treat them as *thous.* Buber uses the term *thou* specifically because it infers that someone is cherished. In the English language, the word *thou* referred to a person of familiarity and importance to us. That is why older English translations of the Bible refer to God as *Thou.* God is cherished, and God calls each of God's children *thou.* When we treat a person as though he or she is not a *thou,* then we engage in an *I-It,* an *I-He,* or an *I-She* relationship. We sense no connection or similarity between us.

The tendency to treat others with little regard is an ongoing problem. For example, we look at a person on a subway, and all we see is that *she* dresses radically, dyes *her* hair a funny color, has an earring protruding from the side of *her* nose, and wears black. *She* is different, and chances are that *she* looks upon us with a similar skepticism and caution. This person becomes some "thing" to look at—a *she*—but not to relate to.

When we are in a hurry or want something to be just "perfect," we often treat store clerks, salespeople, garbage collectors, maintenance workers, employees, the unemployed, the poor, teenagers, senior citizens, and many others as just *hes* or *shes* of little importance. We see them only in terms of the service or function they provide. Thus, we are often guilty of treating others as though their role in life is either to serve us or impede us.

In contrast to the *I-It* relationship, Buber describes the *I-Thou* relationship as a relationship marked by connection and similarity. The person who shares an *I-Thou* relationship with someone enters a relationship in which boundaries overlap. The distinctions between them blur to some extent. When I enter into an *I-Thou* relationship with you, I recognize our connection and treat you as I would treat myself. I ignore our differences while embracing our similarities and connections. To treat the woman on the subway as a *thou*, I must recognize that she has the same desires for uniqueness and independence that I have for my own life. While I may not invite the store clerk to my house for dinner and become best friends, I treat him as an important, worthwhile, and respected person. I make eye contact and smile. My anger with a store clerk should not lead me to belittle, degrade, or attack him. Treating another as a *thou* means treating him or her as a person who shares my human condition.

When I enter into an I-Thou relationship with you, I recognize our connection and treat you as I would treat myself.

The *I-It* relationship is one of separation. The *I-Thou* relationship is one of sharing. The other becomes a whole being who is connected and related to me. One interesting aspect of the *I-Thou* relationship is that I actually become an *I* only in relationship to another person as a *thou*.[2] Through another person's regard, I become a more genuine person in the relationship. My regard for the other person allows him or her to become a more genuine person in relationship with me. The better we know each other, the more deeply we can share. This mutuality allows love to form between two people. Thus, love can only exist between an *I* and a *thou*—between two people who treat each other as important and mutual.

Buber's technical language describes Jesus' call for us to love our neighbors as ourselves. By treating others as objects, we treat them not as ourselves, but as people who are different, unlovable, and unworthy of our love and compassion. When we treat others as *thous,* we form a relationship in which we share a sense of mutual love. We treat people as not only inherently lovable (as though they are worthy of love), but as though they are inherently loved by God, which they are. In simpler terms, we treat our neighbors as ourselves. We *cherish* them.

Think about the last time you treated a stranger with love and respect—as a "thou."

Could you sense God's presence in your actions?

Take time to reflect on this, and to notice what allowed you to be caring.

Buber recognizes the inherent connection between love and the divine realm. He suggests that when we treat another as a *thou*, we are simultaneously addressing the eternal *Thou*: "Every particular *Thou* is a glimpse through to the eternal *Thou*."[3] Every time we treat another person as a *thou*—every time we cherish another person—we connect ourselves with God (the eternal *Thou*) who is the foundation of all true loving relationships. We treat another as a *thou* because that is how God always treats us. Although God would be justified in doing so, God never treats us as anything less than cherished, mutual partners. Since I am always loved by God, I am a person who can love and be loved by others. Without God's love for me and my love for God, I cannot really love myself; nor can I really have any true love for others. Real love only emerges from our relationship with God.

Read John 11:1-44.

What does this passage teach you about love?

The reality of human life is that while God calls us to live in *I-Thou* relationships—in loving relationships—with God, ourselves, and others, we are not very good at maintaining these kinds of relationships. On a spiritual level we may recognize the need to treat others with love, but our human self-focus causes us to treat others as less important than we. Over time, we tend to reduce every *thou* to a *he*, *she*, or *it*. We get married and initially treat our spouse as a cherished mutual partner, but eventually we slip into treating him or her as less important. The challenge in marriage is to recognize our tendency to reduce our spouses to objects and to work continually with God to cherish our spouses. Cherishing others requires a constant but gentle self-examination of ourselves and our relationships.

Merging the words of Jesus in Luke 10:27 with Buber's concepts, we can say that God calls us to live in relationship with others in a way that treats all others as cherished beings. We enhance our ability to treat others in this way whenever we love God and accept God's love for us. We are God's cherished children, and God treats us as mutual partners. Being cherished by God allows us to become who we are—human beings worthy of love and capable of loving others. Firmly rooted in God's love, we can reach out to others and treat them as cherished beings, which offers them the opportunity to reciprocate.

In reality, maintaining fully mutual, cherishing relationships is very difficult. It is less important that we remain in a constant state of mutual love than it is that we honestly recognize how often we treat ourselves or others as inferior. Only by humbly recognizing our propensity to separate, insulate, and isolate ourselves from God can we reconnect with God's love. When we admit to ourselves that we push God away and that we need God's love, then we can begin truly to discover opportunities to treat others as cherished, mutual partners.

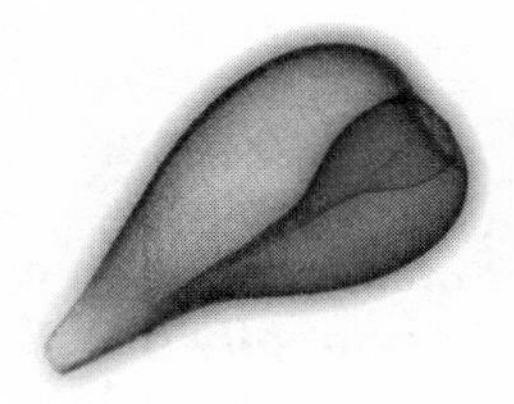

One potential limitation of Buber's concept of *I-Thou* relationships is that we often think of it only with regard to immediate, interpersonal relationships. We cherish only those who are close to us. To be rooted truly in God and God's love, we need to cherish people on three levels of life: the personal, the relational, and the social.

When we admit to ourselves that we push God away and that we need God's love, then we can begin truly to discover opportunities to treat others as cherished, mutual partners.

Personal Cherishing

Before all else, we need to cherish ourselves on a *personal level,* for God calls us to accept our own personal, innate worth. Many of us either underestimate or overestimate our worth. Addicted or abused people often see themselves as bad or worthless. I recall a woman I knew years ago who was in an abusive marriage that she felt helpless to escape. When I asked her why she stayed in the marriage, she told me that no one wanted to hire an older woman who has been out of the work force for years and has two kids. I saw her as beautiful, bright, and competent. She would have had no problem finding work and supporting herself. But she did not believe that she was loved or lovable; her husband's ruthless comments had convinced her that she was worthless. She did not believe herself to be cherished by God or others.

In contrast, overestimating our own self-worth is common among those of us who are overly independent people, especially if we have achieved some level of success or privilege. Sometimes when we gain a certain level of wealth, influence, or notoriety, we may begin to treat ourselves as critically important people. We may see ourselves as particularly competent in a world of incompetent people. Anthony de Mello humorously evokes this attitude with a story:

> *Mother*: "What does your girlfriend like in you?"
> *Son*: "She thinks I'm handsome, talented, clever, and a good dancer."
> *Mother*: "And what do you like about her?"
> *Son*: "She thinks I'm handsome, talented, clever, and a good dancer."[4]

Cherishing ourselves means living in a personally moral way that reminds us of God's love for us and that affirms our worth.

Acclaim and recognition from others can become a spiritual handicap that can interfere with our ability to respond to others with love and compassion because we do not recognize their worth. We do not recognize the gift of Christ's spirit within them.

Our personal morality is related to the extent to which we cherish ourselves. Criticism of our present-day concern with morals and morality fails to understand that morals simply refer to customs and practices that exist to make our lives healthier. I once heard a priest define morality as anything that is "life-giving." He defined immorality as anything that is "life-diminishing." What struck me was that while we often see morals in terms of rules and restrictions, his definition suggests that living a life of personal morality enhances our lives. Cherishing ourselves means living in a personally moral way that reminds us of God's love for us and that affirms our worth. Personal morality means respecting ourselves in a way that gives birth to personal growth, care, and love.

Read 1 Corinthians 6:12-20.

What does this say about how we should treat ourselves and our bodies?

Personal morality, rooted in an awareness of our partnership with God, influences every area of life. From a physical perspective, it leads us to treat our bodies with care and respect. We do not have to live like modern ascetics whose practices obsessively include constant exercise and a no-fat diet. We do not have to look like a twenty-year-old in a beer commercial. Respecting our bodies simply means sleeping, eating, drinking, exercising, and taking care of our bodies with a sense of balance, moderation, and care. We can overdo this regimen just as easily as we can underdo it. As Paul reminds, "Do you not know that your body is a temple of the Holy Spirit within you, which you have from God, and that you are not your own?" (1 Cor. 6:19). Temples do not have to gleam with perfection. Some of the most beautiful churches and temples are beautiful because age, use, and gentle care have made them so. Treating our bodies as temples implies respect and care within balance.

From a sexual perspective, personal morality means acknowledging sex as both a procreative act and a loving act. Using our sexuality carelessly in relationships that are lacking in love detracts from our lives. Promiscuity does not enhance our lives; we treat ourselves as objects to be used by other human objects and others as objects to be used by us.

In what ways have you treated yourself as less than an I?

Take time to reflect on how you can treat yourself more as someone cherished by God.

From a vocational perspective, personal morality means using our careers as vehicles for contribution, self-expression, and creativity in fields that allow us to use our skills. Whether as a carpet layer or a business executive, using our careers solely to attain wealth, acclaim, independence, or security may cause us to drive, abuse, or punish ourselves. Personal morality means allowing our work to *express* our self-worth instead of *establishing* our worth. Our worth derives from God's love.

Relational Cherishing

Besides cherishing ourselves, we need to cherish others on a relational level. We express our innate worth by cherishing others, which in turn enhances our personal sense of being cherished. This level of living moves beyond *personal* morality to *interpersonal* morality.

Cherishing others enlivens not only ourselves but others. Too often we do not realize how readily love can instill a sense of life in others. We generally put conditions on our love of others: They must please us, change for us, measure up to our standards, and embrace certain customs. Yet when we withhold love, we diminish life. The Christmas television program about Rudolph, the red-nosed reindeer, provides a wonderful example of the energy we share when we love others. Rudolph has a terrible crush on a cute little doe named Clarice, but he's very shy. When he finally talks to her and she tells him that she thinks he is cute, Rudolph explodes with joy. He jumps and dances with delight, yelling, "She thinks I'm cute! She thinks I'm cute!" He becomes animated and excited, full of energy and life. Cherishing others can fill people with this kind of life.

Attempting to cherish others leads us to love our neighbors as ourselves. We learn to treat each person we meet with respect, dignity, concern, and compassion. We need to love others not only as we love ourselves, but as we *should* love ourselves. We set standards of love for our treatment of ourselves and of others.

Have you ever had a situation in which the love of another gave you life? a time in which you cared for another, and it gave life to her or him?

Take time to reflect on these and similar instances.

Cherishing others requires us to live out a *compassionate faith*, which essentially means becoming rooted in suffering. We tend to think of compassion as having care and concern for another person. Compassion goes much deeper. Compassion means "sharing our suffering." At its root, *compassion* literally means "suffering with" another person—not only recognizing the pain and struggles of another person but sharing in that suffering.

Anthony de Mello tells a story about shared suffering:

> "My friend isn't back from the battlefield, sir. Request permission to go out and get him."
>
> "Permission refused," said the officer. "I don't want you to risk your life for a man who is probably dead."
>
> The soldier went all the same. Hours later, he returned mortally wounded, carrying the corpse of his friend. The officer was furious. "I told you he was dead. Now I've lost both of you. Tell me, was it worth going out there to bring in a corpse?"
>
> The dying man replied, "Oh, it was, sir. When I got to him, he was still alive. And he said to me, 'Jack, I was sure you'd come.'"[5]

"Through compassion," says Henri Nouwen "it is possible to recognize that the craving for love that [people] feel resides also in our own hearts, that the cruelty that the world knows all too well is also rooted in our own impulses. Through compassion we also sense our hope for forgiveness in our friends' eyes and our hatred in their bitter mouths."[6] Through compassion we not only feel the suffering of others, but we recognize our own suffering in the suffering of other people. Like Jesus, those of us who announce liberty must care not only for our own wounds and the wounds of others, but we must make our wounds a source of healing power. Compassion for others originates in our ability to recognize our own suffering. By knowing our own pains we become more sensitive to the suffering of others.

Those recovering from addictions often discover for the first time that other people experience the same feelings that they thought they alone had felt. Many recovering people have believed that no one else in the world has ever felt as rejected by others as they, nor as misunderstood, scared of the future, and unfairly attacked by life. Prior to their recovery, they had become so emotionally protective that they saw only their own suffering. The fact that other people often saw them as failures without seeing their suffering compounded the problem. In our culture and world, we often become numb to our own suffering and that of others. Treating others as *thous* requires that we recognize their suffering as well as our own.

How well do you respond to suffering?

Are you able to recognize and admit your own suffering?

Are you able to recognize the suffering of others?

As we become more sensitive toward others, we also become more aware of Another's suffering—the divine suffering of God. Andrew Purves, a pastoral theologian, reminds us that the Hebrew Scriptures depict God as compassionate, suffering with the people of Israel. The New Testament portrays God through the ministry of Jesus Christ as suffering and compassionate.[7] Many people today do not believe that God suffers or has compassion for us. Purves asserts that compassion is an integral part of the way God has related with us since the creation of the world, and God continues to have compassion for us.[8]

God suffers with us because God is active in life. God not only sees what is happening in the universe, but God feels it. God experiences our feelings and those of the cosmos. This is what it means to say that God is an immanent, incarnate God. Thus, God shares our joys and our sorrows.

God is not a distant and aloof God who sets the world in motion and now admires it. As Christians, we affirm that God became human, suffered, died, and then overcame death through the Resurrection. In Christ, God not only showed us the depth of love but also taught us how we are to love and live. God treats us as cherished *thous*, for God cares deeply about our lives. It was once said that when we suffer, God is the first one to shed a tear. Our acknowledgment of God's compassion and willingness to suffer with us encourages us to recognize our own suffering and that of others and to reach out in compassion.

Read John 11:1-44 again.

In what ways did Jesus suffer with others?

What does this say about God's suffering?

Donald McNeill, Douglas Morrison, and Henri Nouwen suggest that the compassionate life is a life lived patiently with others.[9] To patiently bear with the suffering of others requires us to be willing to wait with others in their pain and turmoil. While caring for others with compassion may mean helping solve particular problems, we are often too focused on fixing things. We may feel pressure to fix another's problems. Generally people do not want us to fix their problems; they usually want us simply to wait and listen.

How well do you listen to others?

Are you comfortable listening when there seem to be no solutions?

Take time to pray about this and to ask God to guide you in listening to others with growing compassion.

I used to share my struggles with a particular man. He gave me so much advice and offered so many suggestions that I eventually stopped confiding in him. I just wanted someone to listen patiently to me, while I sought the best solutions for myself. As McNeill and his colleagues say, "Patience involves staying with it, living it through, listening carefully to what presents itself to us here and now."[10]

The prophet Micah's urgings to the Israelites seems to reflect this compassionate perspective, "[God] has told you, O mortal, what is good; and what does the Lord require of you but to do justice, and to love kindness, and to walk humbly with your God?" (6:8). Micah urges us to treat others with respect, even if they do not treat us in the same way; to act with humility by listening to God in everything; to treat others with kindness by being compassionate, gentle, and tender; to respond to others from our heart by acting justly in all circumstances. When we do all of these things, we treat others as *thous*, and at the same time we enhance our own being. We give life to others and to ourselves.

Social and Global Cherishing

A third way in which God calls us to cherish others is on the *social and global level.* God calls us to accept ourselves and others as cherished beings and to extend this attitude into social and global spheres. Compassion must move beyond the personal and interpersonal.We are called upon to give life not only to those we know but also to those we do not know—the poor, the hungry, the homeless, those seeking refuge, those seeking equality, and those seeking compassion. We call this avenue of compassion social morality.

We are called upon to give life not only to those we know but also to those we do not know—the poor, the hungry, the homeless, those seeking refuge, those seeking equality, and those seeking compassion.

With the increasing desire for spiritual growth, we tend to make spirituality exclusively private and individual. When we say, "You know, I worship *my* God in *my* way," we create God instead of the other way around. Many people excel in personal prayer and meditation, while ignoring the plight of those around them. But spirituality goes hand in hand with justice, and faith is not separate from compassion. As the writer of James reminds us, "For just as the body without the spirit is dead, so faith without works is also dead" (2:26). A failure to recognize the plight of those we do not know bears witness to a stunted and immature faith.

Robert McAfee Brown calls the split we create between spirituality and social justice (or liberation) the "Great Fallacy." He says the term *liberation* describes the attempt to wipe out oppressive structures that cause disadvantaged lives, while the term *spirituality* describes a state of being in which "spiritual exercises" help us connect with a Reality, or God.[11] While many people consider the term *liberation* an emotionally charged theological and political term, we should remember that liberation simply means offering freedom to those who do not have it. As Americans we cherish freedom and the process of offering opportunities for this freedom to those constrained by political, economic, or social situations.

True spirituality leads to acts of liberation, justice, and compassion on social and global scales.

The Great Fallacy arises when we fail to see the connection between liberation and spirituality.[12] True spirituality leads to acts of liberation, justice, and compassion on social and global scales. Compassionate liberation enhances our spirituality and reconnects our works and faith. The prophet Micah admonishes us to unite humility, kindness, and justice—to make the connection between openness to God and display of compassion to others. (See Micah 6:8.) He speaks of justice, kindness, and humility on a social level as well as a personal and interpersonal level. His social prophecies include all people.

How do you view the connection between personal and social morality?

Can you separate the two?

Take time to reflect on this issue.

I first recognized the connection between spirituality and social justice as a seminary student while reading a biography of Mahatma Gandhi. I was supposed to have been studying for a church history exam, but I just could not put the biography down. Gandhi was a remarkable man primarily because he naturally lived out the *I-Thou* relationships that Martin Buber described. Gandhi's strong and vibrant prayer life led him not only to treat the people he knew with great respect, deference, and care but to care deeply about the welfare of all people in India, whether Christian, Muslim, Buddhist, Sikh, or Hindu.

Those who disagreed with Gandhi and criticized him to his face often found his humble responses disarming. He would thank them for their comments and integrate their concerns into his own. He demonstrated a radical openness to God. At one point his attempts to secure India's independence nonviolently seemed to be on the verge of collapsing into violent conflict. Instead of allowing the struggle for independence to become violent, Gandhi went on a hunger strike until all of the Indian people united once again in a peaceful revolution.

How have your own faith and spirituality led you to care for those you do not know?

Talk with God about how you can increase your care for the oppressed, the poor, and the hungry.

Before embarking on a campaign of civil disobedience, Gandhi could often be found in prayer. Sometimes he waited in prayer for days or weeks but just as often for months. Gandhi always based his actions upon his relationship with God, and he allowed the love of that relationship to flow outward into his love for all those suffering from oppression. His relationship with God enabled him to treat his friends and enemies with equal love and respect.

Today we often treat social justice issues as part of a conservative-liberal battle in which one side or the other must lose. In such a struggle, we all lose. God is not conservative or liberal or anything else. God supports all people and wants all people to share in life. Spirituality must always seek a balance that includes personal and social humility.

The real problem that causes us to disconnect faith from justice is that we tend to approach social issues from a grounding in political tradition instead of Christian tradition. "Hot" topics such as poverty, homosexuality, abortion, education, gun control, and economic inequality are particularly divisive.

Our strong adherence to political traditions may cause us to forget our need to adhere even more strongly to the deeper Christian tradition that requires a compassionate approach to all of life. This grounding in compassion calls us to be effusive and outgoing in our love of family, friends, the poor, and the oppressed at times; but it also calls us at times to be tough in our love of these same people. The true guide is God—not political expediency, efficiency, or rhetoric. Political traditions do not arise out of an *I-Thou* orientation. Even well-meaning political traditions arise from a desire to gain and maintain power, an *I-It* orientation. They tend to treat enemies and even allies as objects that either aid or hinder their "fight." The same roots nurture social strife, hunger, and violence. Treating others as objects promotes separation through racism, sexism, elitism, and any other kind of "-ism" that separates people. All are social manifestations of the *I-It* relationship.

To be Christian means we follow Christian traditions that emphasize compassion and that assist us in our adherence to political traditions and ideas to guide us. Whatever our political party, we must first be Christians, looking upon others from an *I-Thou* perspective. We must always connect spirituality and social justice by rooting ourselves in our relationship with God.

Deep compassionate faith extends to all levels of life: for ourselves on the personal level, for others on a relational level, and for all people on social and global levels. The faith journey is a journey of love that begins and ends with a love of God, while teaching us the importance of deepening our love for ourselves and for others continually. As we walk along the journey of faith, we have to resist the temptation to give in to distrust, cynicism, hatred, contempt, and lack of compassion. Instead, we choose to accept God's invitation to share in the eternal *I-Thou* relationship that evokes in us a loving and compassionate faith.

Read Galatians 3:23-29.

What does this passage say about the ways humanity finds issues to divide it instead of seeking unity?

How does it say God regards you?

Notes

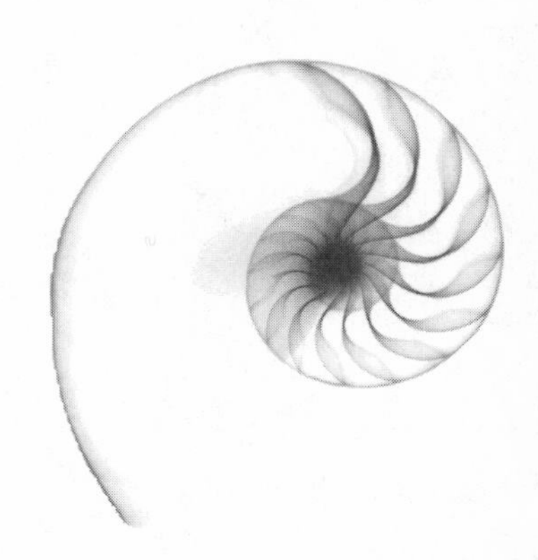

CHAPTER ONE: QUESTIONS OF FAITH

1. For more on the different kinds of belief, refer to John Macquarrie, *In Search of Humanity: A Theological and Philosophical Approach* (New York: Crossroad, 1989), 158–171.

2. Adrian van Kaam calls this decision the *foundational formation decision.* He notes that it entails choosing either to believe in the meaningfulness or in the meaninglessness of our life and formation. For more on this, see Adrian van Kaam, *Fundamental Formation: Formative Spirituality,* vol. 1 (New York: Crossroad, 1989), 221.

3. Bonhoeffer actually states, "Only he who believes is obedient, and only he who is obedient believes." Substituting *listen* for *obedient* makes sense since the root of obedience is *audire,* which means "to hear." Thus, being obedient literally means to listen or to hear. In terms of faith we might say that being obedient means listening to or hearing God and then acting on what we hear. For more on Bonhoeffer's thoughts, refer to Dietrich Bonhoeffer, *The Cost of Discipleship* (New York: Macmillan, Collier Books, 1963), 69.

4. John Calvin, *The Institutes of Christian Religion,* ed. Tony Lane and Hilary Osborne (Grand Rapids: Baker Book House, 1987), 217.

5. Terry A. Anderson, *Den of Lions: Memoirs of Seven Years* (New York: Crown Publishers, Inc., 1993), 75.

6. Ibid.

CHAPTER TWO: EXPECTATIONS

1. Anthony de Mello, *The Song of the Bird* (New York: Doubleday, Image Books, 1984), 153.

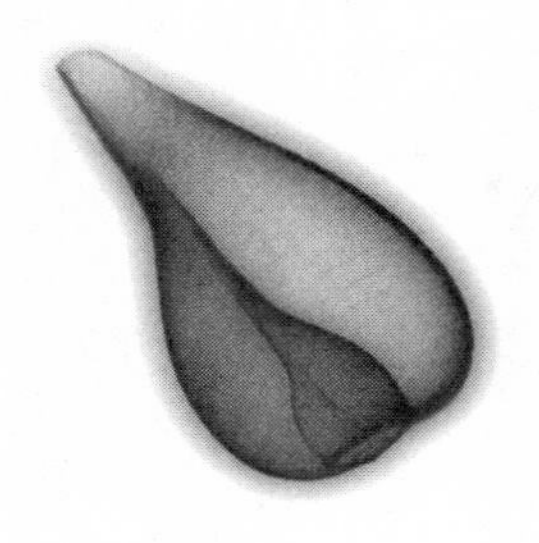

2. Adrian van Kaam, *The Transcendent Self: Formative Spirituality of the Middle, Early, and Later Years of Life* (Pittsburgh, Penn.: Epiphany Association, 1991), 8. This work explores the connection between "midlife crises" and transcendence crises, as well as how all periods of crisis become times of transcendence crisis.

3. Hannah Hurnard, *Hinds' Feet on High Places* (Wheaton, Ill.: Tyndale House, Living Books, 1986), 82.

4. Ibid.

5. Susan Annette Muto, *Pathways of Spiritual Living* (Petersham, Mass.: St. Bede's Publications, 1984), 44–45.

6. Carolyn Gratton, *The Art of Spiritual Guidance: A Contemporary Approach to Growing in the Spirit* (New York: Crossroad, 1992), 108.

7. David Steindl-Rast, *Gratefulness, the Heart of Prayer: An Approach to Life in Fullness* (New York: Paulist Press, 1984), 9.

8. Adrian van Kaam does an excellent study on the need to cultivate wonder instead of curiosity in education. He comments that in our overly functional culture, we have substituted scientific curiosity for wonder, and as a result we tend to satisfy our curiosity by dissecting and pulling things apart. Wonder appreciates things in their fullness while recognizing the connections between and among them. For more on this, refer to Adrian van Kaam, "Education to Originality," *Foundations for Personality Study* (Denville, N.J.: Dimension Books, Inc., 1983), 278–87.

9. Steindl-Rast, *Gratefulness, the Heart of Prayer,* 9.

10. Wade Clark Roof, *A Generation of Seekers: The Spiritual Journeys of the Baby Boom Generation* (San Francisco: HarperSanFrancisco, 1993), 184.

11. Robert N. Bellah and his colleagues have noted that strong individualistic tendencies have marked the social and political history and life of the American character since the earliest colonization of North America by those seeking personal religious freedom. Therefore, it is natural that at times Americans tend to become overly individualistic in their spiritual philosophies. For more on individualism, see Robert N. Bellah, Richard Madsen, William M. Sullivan, Ann Swidler, and Steven M. Tipton, *Habits of the Heart: Individualism and Commitment in American Life,* rev. ed. (San Francisco: Harper & Row, 1985).

12. Gratton, *The Art of Spiritual Guidance,* 71.

13. For a more thorough discussion on traditions, see Adrian van Kaam, *Traditional Formation: Formative Spirituality,* vol. 5 (New York: Crossroad, 1992).

CHAPTER THREE: HUMBLE BEGINNINGS

1. C. S. Lewis, *The Screwtape Letters* (New York: Bantam Books, 1982), 22.

2. Ernest Becker, *The Denial of Death* (New York: Macmillan, Free Press, 1973), 50.

3. Van Kaam, *Fundamental Formation,* 87–89, 261, 294–95.

4. Thomas R. Kelly, *A Testament of Devotion* (New York: Harper & Row, 1941), 62.

5. Ibid., 61.

6. The discipline of formative spirituality identifies humility with the disposition of openness. Thus, when we are humble our hearts are open to God or (in the language of formative spirituality) to the formation mystery. As van Kaam states, humility is a "relaxed openness to who we are foundationally as a gift of the *formation mystery,* as a vulnerable composite of consonant and dissonant dispositions, directives, and images in mutual dialogue with one another." Our humility opens us at a foundational level to who God created us to be—vulnerable human beings connected to God who are in profound dialogue with each other. For more on this, refer to Adrian van Kaam, *Human Formation: Formative Spirituality,* vol. 2 (New York: Crossroad, 1989), 134–35.

7. For more on the power of memory and anticipation to shape not only who we are, but also the choices we make and the circumstances we face, see van Kaam, *Fundamental Formation,* 108–164.

8. Ron Rosenbaum, "Staring into the Heart of the Heart of Darkness," *The New York Times Magazine* (4 June 1995): 40–41.

9. Lewis, *The Screwtape Letters,* 5.

10. *Pittsburgh Post-Gazette* (Pittsburgh, Penn.), 13 October 1994.

11. Gerald G. May, *Will and Spirit: A Contemplative Psychology* (San Francisco: Harper & Row, 1982), 6.

12. Adrian van Kaam, *Religion and Personality* (Denville, N. J.: Dimension Books, 1980), 98–101.

13. Anthony de Mello, *Taking Flight: A Book of Story Meditations* (New York: Doubleday, 1988), 186.

14. Paul Tillich, *The Shaking of the Foundations* (New York: Charles Scribner's Sons, 1948), 59.

15. Jean-Pierre de Caussade, *The Sacrament of the Present Moment,* trans. Kitty Muggeridge (San Francisco: HarperSan-Francisco, 1982), 15.

16. Lewis, *The Screwtape Letters*, 61.

CHAPTER FOUR: SPEAKING AND LISTENING

1. Richard J. Foster, *Prayer: Finding the Heart's True Home* (San Francisco: HarperSanFrancisco, 1992).

2. Hans Urs von Balthasar, *Prayer*, trans. Graham Harrison (San Francisco: Ignatius Press, 1986), 14.

3. De Mello, *Taking Flight,* 162.

4. Paul Tillich, *The Eternal Now* (New York: Charles Scribner's Sons, 1963), 52.

5. Ibid., 56.

6. Karen Armstrong, *A History of God: The 4,000-Year Quest of Judaism, Christianity and Islam* (New York: Alfred A. Knopf, 1993), 98-99.

7. Agnes Sanford, *The Healing Light* (New York: Ballantine Books, 1983), 3.

8. Van Kaam, *Fundamental Formation,* xvii–xxi, and Adrian van Kaam, *Formation of the Human Heart: Formative Spirituality,* vol. 3 (New York: Crossroad, 1986), 360–61.

9. Brother Lawrence, *The Practice of the Presence of God,* ed. Hal M. Helms, trans. Robert J. Edmonson (Orleans, Mass.: Paraclete Press, 1985), 87.

10. Ibid., 89–90.

11. Tillich, *The Eternal Now,* 86.

CHAPTER FIVE: CONFESSION AND GRACE

1. John B. Cobb Jr., *Praying for Jennifer: An Exploration of Intercessory Prayer in Story Form* (Nashville, Tenn.: The Upper Room, 1985).

2. Ibid., 18.

3. Ibid., 21.

4. Calvin, *The Institutes of Christian Religion,* 69.

5. Macquarrie, *In Search of Humanity,* 153.

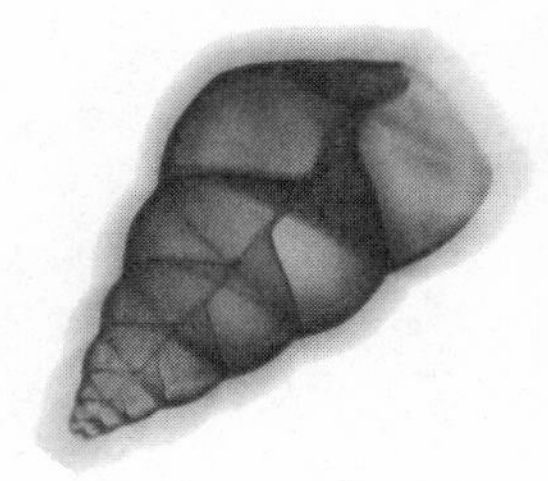

6. Paul Tillich, *The Essential Tillich: An Anthology of the Writings of Paul Tillich,* ed. F. Forrester Church (New York: Macmillan, Collier Books, 1987), 165.

7. Ibid., 166.

8. Ibid., 166–67.

9. This personal confession touched my own life so deeply that I used it as a basis for my doctoral dissertation. For more on this, see N. Graham Standish, *From Individualistic to Communal Spirituality: Nurturing Spiritual Formation through Commitment, Confession, Confirmation, and Community* (Ann Arbor, Mich.: University Microfilms International, 1995), 12.

10. Richard J. Foster, *Celebration of Discipline: The Path to Spiritual Growth*, rev. ed. (San Francisco: Harper & Row, 1988), 153.

11. Dietrich Bonhoeffer, *Life Together,* trans. John W. Doberstein (San Francisco: Harper & Row, 1954), 111.

12. Bonhoeffer, *The Cost of Discipleship,* 47.

CHAPTER SIX: COMMITMENT AND COMMUNITY

1. For a wonderful discussion of the rise of individual approaches to understanding God, see Karen Armstrong, *History of God,* 293–376.

2. Bellah, *Habits of the Heart*, 142–47.

3. Ibid., 146.

4. Ibid., 82.

5. Leo N. Miletich, "Sleepless in El Paso," *Newsweek*, 5 July 1995, 14.

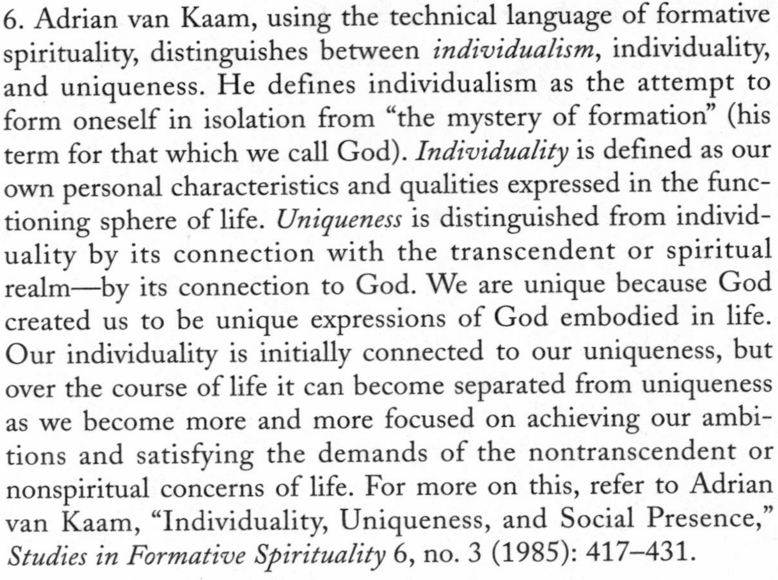

6. Adrian van Kaam, using the technical language of formative spirituality, distinguishes between *individualism*, individuality, and uniqueness. He defines individualism as the attempt to form oneself in isolation from "the mystery of formation" (his term for that which we call God). *Individuality* is defined as our own personal characteristics and qualities expressed in the functioning sphere of life. *Uniqueness* is distinguished from individuality by its connection with the transcendent or spiritual realm—by its connection to God. We are unique because God created us to be unique expressions of God embodied in life. Our individuality is initially connected to our uniqueness, but over the course of life it can become separated from uniqueness as we become more and more focused on achieving our ambitions and satisfying the demands of the nontranscendent or nonspiritual concerns of life. For more on this, refer to Adrian van Kaam, "Individuality, Uniqueness, and Social Presence," *Studies in Formative Spirituality* 6, no. 3 (1985): 417–431.

7. Van Kaam, *Traditional Formation,* vol. 5, 181.

8. Eberhard Arnold, *God's Revolution: The Witness of Eberhard Arnold,* ed. Hutterian Society of Brothers and John Howard Yoder (New York: Paulist Press, 1984), 47.

9. Van Kaam, "Formation Anthropology, Formation Tradition, and Human Nature," *Studies in Formative Spirituality* 12, no. 1 (1991): 10–11.

10. For a more detailed discussion on form and faith traditions, refer to Adrian van Kaam, *Traditional Formation*, 1–32.

11. Van Kaam calls these ranking systems *form traditional pyramids.* This term connotes that we place the most influential traditions at our base and the least influential at the apex. Thus, the traditions near or at the base bear a stronger influence on our lives, and on all of the less foundational traditions. For more on this, please refer to van Kaam, *Traditional Formation,* 34–45.

12. Roof, *A Generation of Seekers,* 184.

13. Macquarrie, *In Search of Humanity,* 141–42.

14. Kelly, *A Testament of Devotion,* 77–79.

15. Ibid., 84.

16. Bonhoeffer, *Life Together,* 34–39.

17. Ibid., 35.

CHAPTER SEVEN: THANKFUL LIVING

1. In my own training as a therapist, I was taught always to offer a sense of hope to my clients—a sense that improvement and change is always possible. For a good discussion on the importance of instilling hope in therapy, refer to Richard A. Wells, *Planned Short-Term Treatment* (New York: MacMillan, Free Press, 1982), 85–88.

2. Gail Sheehy, *Pathfinders: Overcoming the Crises of Adult Life and Finding Your Own Path to Well-Being* (New York: William Morrow and Company, Inc., 1981), 10–23.

3. Ellen K. McCormack, *Moving from Anger to Gratitude: The Formative Power of an Empathic Encounter* (Ann Arbor, Mich.: University Microfilms International, 1997).

4. Adrian van Kaam and Susan Muto, *The Power of Appreciation: A New Approach to Personal and Relational Healing* (New York: Crossroad, 1993), 21–24.

5. Ibid., 21.

6. Evelyn Underhill, *Life as Prayer and Other Writings of Evelyn Underhill,* ed. Lucy Menzies (Harrisburg, Penn.: Morehouse Publishing, 1991), 55.

7. Paul Ricoeur, *Interpretation Theory: Discourse and the Surplus of Meaning* (Fort Worth, Tex.: Texas Christian University Press, 1976), 54–57.

8. Ibid., 57–63.

9. Horace Bushnell, *Sermons*, ed. Conrad Cherry (New York: Paulist Press, 1985), 37.

10. Ibid., 51–52.

11. Tillich, *The Eternal Now,* 179.

12. Thomas à Kempis, *The Imitation of Christ,* trans. William C. Creasy (Notre Dame, Ind.: Ave Maria Press, 1989), 76.

13. Steindl-Rast, *Gratefulness, the Heart of Prayer,* 9-10.

14. Tillich, *The Eternal Now,* 174–76.

CHAPTER EIGHT: A COMPASSIONATE FAITH

1. Martin Buber, *I and Thou,* 2nd ed., trans. Ronald Gregor Smith (New York: Charles Scribner's Sons, 1958), 3. In translating this

book, the term *thou* has been used instead of the common English pronoun *you*. Rather than being an archaic term often associated with older versions of the Bible, *thou* is a very specific term. Like German and French, English used to have a more familiar term for the second person singular, and that was *thou*. Today we refer to everyone in the second person as *you*, but in older English a person who was familiar and intimate was referred to as *thou*. In using the term *thou*, Buber emphasizes the intimacy among people.

2. Ibid., 11.

3. Ibid., 75.

4. De Mello, *Taking Flight,* 150.

5. Ibid., 147.

6. Henri J. M. Nouwen, *The Wounded Healer: Ministry in Contemporary Society* (Garden City, N.Y.: Doubleday, Image Books, 1979), 41.

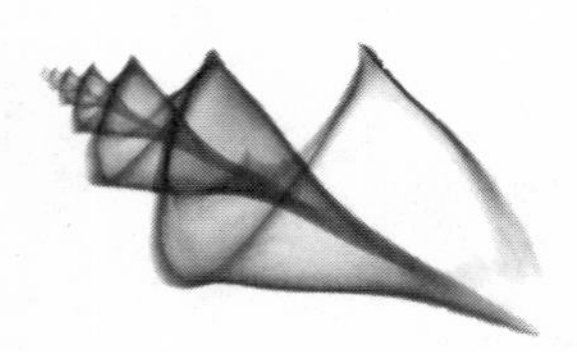

7. Andrew Purves, *The Search for Compassion: Spirituality and Ministry* (Louisville, Ky.: Westminster: John Knox Press, 1989), 63–73.

8. Ibid., 76.

9. Donald P. McNeill, Douglas A. Morrison, and Henri J. M. Nouwen, *Compassion: A Reflection on the Christian Life* (Garden City, N.Y.: Doubleday, Image Books, 1983), 92.

10. Ibid., 93.

11. Robert McAfee Brown, *Spirituality and Liberation: Overcoming the Great Fallacy* (Philadelphia, Penn.: Westminster Press, 1988), 16–17.

12. Ibid., 25 and following.

About the Author

DR. STANDISH is pastor of Calvin Presbyterian Church in Zelienople, Pennsylvania. He has degrees in psychology and social work from Roanoke College and the University of Pittsburgh, and in divinity from Pittsburgh Theological Seminary. He also has a Ph.D. in formative spirituality from Dusquesne University. He is a teacher and retreat leader in the field of spiritual formation and has served as a pastoral counselor, drug and alcohol therapist, and mental health therapist.

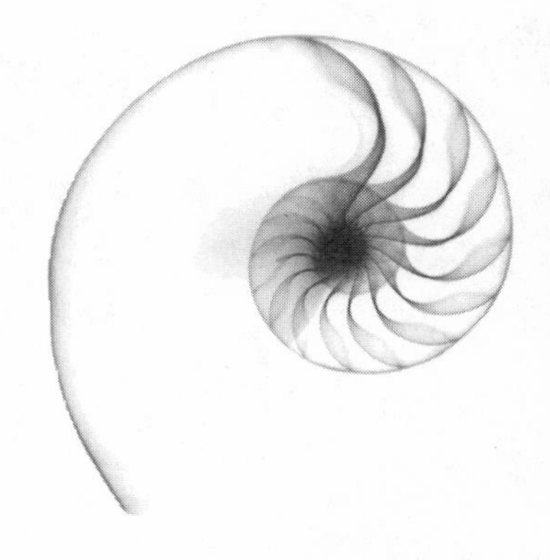